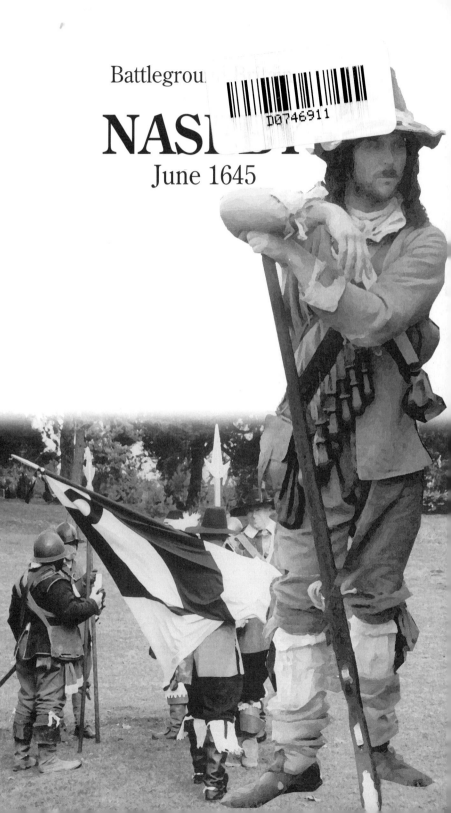

Battlegrou...

NAS[...]
June 1645

D0746911

With the continued expansion of the Battleground series a **Battleground Series Club** has been formed to benefit the reader. The purpose of the Club is to keep members informed of new titles and to offer many other reader-benefits. Membership is free and by registering an interest you can help us predict print runs and thus assist us in maintaining the quality and prices at their present levels.

Please call the office 01226 734555, or send your name and address along with a request for more information to:

Battleground Series Club Pen & Sword Books Ltd,
47 Church Street, Barnsley, South Yorkshire S70 2AS

Previous page: members of The Sealed Knot, officers of Prince Rupert's Blew Regiment of Foote, on exercise at Stowe Gardens, Buckinghamshire.

Parliamentarian musketeer: a member of the English Civil War Society.

Battleground Britain

NASEBY
June 1645

Martin Marix Evans,
Peter Burton and Michael Westaway

LEO COOPER

First published in 2002
by LEO COOPER
an imprint of
Pen & Sword Books Ltd
47 Church Street, Barnsley, South Yorkshire S70 2AS

Copyright © Martin Marix Evans, Peter Burton and Michael Westaway
2002
Landscape photographs by Martin Marix Evans, © 2002

ISBN 0 85052 871 2

A CIP catalogue of this book is available from the British Library

Printed by CPI UK

The Publishers would like to acknowledge the help given by Daniel Millum of the **Royal Armouries** for permission to reproduce photographs of museum exhibits. Also David Hunt and Simon Lister of the **English Civil War Society** for the loan of photographs depicting Society members during re-enactment (credited ECWS).

CONTENTS

LIST OF MAPS

Producing a Battleground Europe volume on events of the seventeenth century is rather different from covering more recent wars. The documentary evidence is sparse and official military reports in the modern sense are lacking entirely. Those reports of the Civil War in England that do exist are essentially letters written as may please the writer at the time. They lack formal structure, make no attempt to be objective, are vague as to timing and neglect narrative sequence. Some, of course, are better than others, but their

An image of an autocratic king; Charles I holds court. He ruled for many years without summoning Parliament and was suspected of Roman Catholic sympathies.

use involves creative reconstruction by the historian and thus affords considerable room for alternative interpretation and wishful thinking.

Maps were rare at the time and are yet rarer today. In the case of Naseby one pre-war map survives, that of the parish as it was in 1630. Road maps did not exist, but Saxton and Speed had made county maps that showed hills and bridges and roads began to appear on maps in the next forty years, so there is some contemporary evidence of where men might have marched and wagons been driven.

The countryside today bears no resemblance at all to the Northamptonshire of 1645, save for the hills. The rivers of the time have been tamed by the creation of canals and their water supply arrangements, and the land alongside them is largely drained by systems installed since then. Modern roads, much though we may grumble about them, bear little relation to the highways of the seventeenth century other than the routes they follow. The first attempt since Roman times to establish state control for long-distance travel was made with an Act of 1555. It was ineffectual. The first turnpike roads were set up after the war. Most of the travellers went on foot; people, cattle and geese alike. A few travelled on horseback. Yet fewer journeyed by bone-shaking cart or coach which was miserably uncomfortable in fine weather and hellish in the wet. Finally, the landscape itself was vastly different. In the area with which we are concerned in this book few villages had been enclosed and the medieval open fields were still the norm, so that, with the exception of the Royal Forests of Whittlewood, Salcey and Rockingham to the south and east of the Naseby campaign territory, the country was open, treeless and without hedges save at parish boundaries. It is also worth remembering that the western flank of Rockingham Forest was marked by the Northampton to Market Harborough road and that the Whittlewood Forest spread across the land between the River Ouse in the south and the River Tove on the approach to Northampton, areas largely absent from the story that follows, but confining the action to the territory discussed here.

So, there are few writings, fewer maps and the whole place looks different. In the circumstances we had better explain how we came to set down what follows, for it may seem curious that we dare say anything at all!

This book is founded in the terrain. Two of the authors were born and grew up in the principal parishes involved. They have both taken an interest in the battle since their boyhood and have more recently spent day after day examining the ground with their metal detectors thanks to the kind permission granted by neighbourly landowners. In addition they have walked, and the third member of the group, the scribe, has walked with them over all the key locations, again by permission of tolerant farmers who look kindly on their curious behaviour. It is with the mapping of finds of shot, coins and equipment and the appreciation of the landscape itself that the work begins.

Second, what written evidence there is has been examined carefully in the light of the landscape research. The few first-hand reports, the immediately proximate secondary accounts and the relatively close histories, within a survivor's lifetime, have been studied closely, as have training manuals of the time. To that has been added the examination of the work of noted military historians. This has all been tested against the empirical evidence of the ground and its contents.

The result is anything but certainty. Pulling together the facts, reports and opinions leads to an arguably persuasive account of events, but it is not a truth. Alternatives are possible and readers will find in the book, we trust, all the material required to build them in contradiction to what we offer. Further, new finds are possible and ideas may be readjusted at some future time.

The Battle of Naseby dealt a fatal blow to the Royalist cause in the First Civil War and can reasonably be ranked with just two other battles on English soil, Hastings and Bosworth, as the great, pivotal fights in British history. That its location should be so poorly known and the sequence of events in the landscape so difficult to discover is a situation demanding correction. One of the earliest researchers of the battlefield was Edward Fitzgerald, whose family had land here at the enclosure of 1820, including Cloister, Mill and Lodge Hills, the area of the Parliamentarian lines at the start of the battle. He carried out a lively correspondence with Thomas Carlyle who wrote to him on 18 September 1842, saying:

'Few spots of ground in all the world are memorabler to an Englishman. We could still very well stand a good little book on Naseby!'

And again on 10 October:

'There ought to be a correct, complete, and every way right and authentic Essay, or little Book, written about Naseby as it now is and as it then seems to have been – with the utmost possible distinctness, succinctness, energy, accuracy and available talent of every sort: I leave you to consider, whether

8

The stereotype of fun-loving Cavaliers (Royalists) versus grim Puritans (Parliamentarians) is excessively simplified. Both sides were internally divided by religious and political difference.

the actual Owner and Heaven's-Steward of Naseby ought to have no hand in that!'

Fitzgerald failed to rise to the bait. Carlyle lays down a challenge to which few, if any, are equal. This volume is, at best, another step along the way and its authors deny any claim to the virtues rehearsed by Carlyle, although two of them could rank as among actual owners but might jib at being classed as Heaven's-Stewards!

The book begins with a brief summary of the developing situation in the months preceding the battle and, because few readers can be expected to be familiar with the weapons and mode of warfare of the time, a short description is given of them. In order to avoid cluttering up the text with travel data, the next four chapters of the book give a narrative account closely related to the landscape. The landscape itself, then and today, is illustrated with maps and photographs. Troop positions and movements shown are, of necessity, only approximate. Finally, chapter six follows the same sequence with detailed travelling advice presented in such as way as to allow readers to plan their own routes on their own maps to suit their own needs. At the time of writing the battlefield has no facilities for visitors and few public footpaths, but this book should enable people to enjoy a rewarding and exciting visit none the less and, should access improve in the future, some of the views now only available in the photographs will be accessible by all. That the entire battlefield should be open to visitors is a circumstance much to be desired and for which the authors are working. In the meantime this is the best we can offer.

In addition to the books referred to in the text and listed in the references section, material has been reproduced by courtesy of the Bodleian Library, Oxford, the Suffolk County Council, the Northamptonshire Record Society and the Northamptonshire County Council. Attributions are made in the captions together with, where possible, reference numbers that will permit interested readers to view the originals or obtain copies for their own use. Ordnance Survey mapping is Crown copyright. We have also received valuable help from Alastair Bantock, Tom Burton, who made the aerial photographs possible to take, Glenn Foard and Chris Scott, none of whom can be held responsible for any shortcomings of the work.

Martin Marix Evans, Silverstone
Peter Burton, Sibbertoft
Michael Westaway, Naseby
DECEMBER 2001

Pistols were the weapon of the cavalry, and usually carried in pairs.
ROYAL ARMOURIES, LEEDS

Wheellock pistol. The cocking piece holds a slither of pyrite, which is lowered against a serated edge of the wheel. The wheel (wound up by a spanner) when the trigger is squeezed, spins against the pyrite causing sparks which, in turn, ignite the powder.

The stock of this flintlock appears to have been originally intended for a wheellock mechanism, as does the lock plate.

This flintlock was made by a London gunsmith who produced arms for the Paliamentarians. This design would carry on into the next century.

Chapter 1

EARLY 1645 – THE WAR, THE ARMIES AND THE TERRAIN

At the outset of 1645 the territory of England was, broadly speaking, divided between the Royalists in the Midlands and the west with headquarters in Oxford and the Parliamentarians in the south and east with headquarters in London, but it is more helpful to regard this division as being between spheres of influence than terrain controlled. There was no front line as such. The Eastern Association, the grouping of the counties of Norfolk, Suffolk, Essex, Hertfordshire, Cambridgeshire, Huntingdonshire and Lincolnshire, was firm Parliament country and, with his victory at Lostwithiel in Cornwall in August 1644, Charles I had secured the West Country, although Taunton and Gloucester were in Parliamentary hands. In the north the Royalists had suffered a severe defeat at Marston Moor in July 1644 where only the fall of night enabled them to save a significant part of their forces and so York and the control of the north was lost to them. Notwithstanding, these territorial dominions still contained pepperings of opposition garrisons in towns, castles or houses and considerable stretches of no man's land where, for the time being at least, the inhabitants were happily free of either side. Further, tolerance was often extended to people of opposite loyalty in a given area. In the staunchly Parliamentarian country of

King Charles I

Northamptonshire, at Maidwell, east of Naseby, the Royalist Sir William Haselwood refrained from any active expression of his views and went unmolested.

The defeat in the west put Parliament in fear of an attack on London so they gathered three armies, those of the Earl of

Manchester, Sir William Waller and the Earl of Essex, at Baskingstoke in Hampshire. The King on his part was also fearful for the security of his outposts; Basing House near Basingstoke, Donnington Castle near Newbury in Berkshire and Banbury, north of Oxford, all of which were besieged. Should these fall Oxford itself would be endangered. The concentration of Parliamentary armies prevented any relief of Basing House and Banbury was freed from investment on 25 October. Thus it was that, on 27 October, 1644, the Royalists found themselves facing their enemies on two fronts, east and west, between Newbury and Donnington. The Parliamentarians failed to spring their trap and the King escaped to Oxford, later returning reinforced to succeed in resupplying both Donnington Castle and Basing House before winter set in.

In the New Year, 1645, the Royalists had some cause for cheerfulness. Their army in the west, under Lord Goring, was sound and they had a second army, mainly artillery and infantry, at Oxford. At the same time their enemies were clearly in considerable disarray. The problem was to decide what to do, and here, in the Royalist high command, they faced their greatest problem; infirmity of purpose. Charles had made his nephew, Prince Rupert of the Rhine, Commander-in-Chief of his army during the Newbury campaign, but he continued to heed the council of his courtiers and in particular that of his Secretary of State, Lord Digby. Moreover, Charles would shortly negate Rupert's supremacy in command by giving Goring an independent mission in the west. However, it was decided that they should retake control of the north country and, as a preliminary, relieve Chester which was besieged by Sir William Brereton.

Prince Rupert

For Parliament nothing less than a total reorganization of their military power would suffice after the fiasco of Newbury. In addition to the mutual rivalry of the commanders of their various armies, religious difference split them. The Earl of Manchester not only accused Oliver Cromwell of errors in his handling of the cavalry at Newbury, but of opposing the replacement of the established church with a Presbyterian structure. In both he had a case. Cromwell openly advocated independent congregations free of hierarchical rule, but in military matters saw the need for a single command structure. The existing Parliamentarian armies were derived from the traditional county militia at the head of which it was natural to find the earls of Essex and Manchester and, while the Eastern Association was an example of the strength that alliance could give, the idea of a national force funded centrally was as distasteful to the Association as to the other militia. It was therefore only as the outcome of subtle and skilful political work that the two vital pieces of legislation were enacted. The Self-Denying Ordinance prevented a person holding both a political and a military position. You were either an officer in the army or you were in Parliament. This, of course, had the effect of ejecting both Essex and Manchester from the army as, being members of the House of Lords, they were inevitably in Parliament. The second measure, taken a month later in December 1644, was the New Model Ordinance, creating a single army out of the three which had failed at Newbury. Sir Thomas Fairfax was appointed to command the army and Cromwell was given temporary leave to remain in service. Fairfax was responsible to the executive Committee for Both Kingdoms (sometimes known as the Derby House Committee) which had been set up in February 1644 to control the war against the King in both England and Scotland. It was made up of four Scottish commissioners, seven members of the House of Lords and

Sir Thomas Fairfax

fourteen of the House of Commons; an arrangement no more likely to generate clear orders than the lobbying courtiers and soldiers surrounding the King.

The New Model Army was planned to have twelve regiments of foot each of 1,200 men, eleven of horse with 600 men and ten of dragoons with 100 men; a total of 22,000 men. By the end of March 1645 all the officers had been appointed by Fairfax and his second-in-command Major General Philip Skippon was approved by Parliament. Equipment and supplies were pouring in during April. This had the makings of a formidable opponent to the King, but it was as yet untried as a whole. The Royalists held it in contempt, failing to recognise that at least half of the men were battle-hardened infantry with a debt of defeat to repay and that the cavalry were previously successful troops.

The Foot

The fighting men of both sides were alike in armament and tactics. Footsoldiers were either pikemen or musketeers. The pike was an ancient weapon, at this time nearing the end of its operational usefulness, while the musket had been in regular use for less than a century. The equipment and drilling of soldiers was the subject of Gervase Markham's *The Souldier's Accidence*, published in 1625 and quoted extensively by Francis Grose in his *Military Antiquities* which was first published in 1786 and of which a new edition, from which much of what follows in text and illustration is taken, appeared in 1812. Markham says:

'... all his pikemen shall have good combe-caps [morions] for their heads, well lined with quilted caps, curaces for their bodies of nimble and good mould, being high pike proof; large and well compact gordgetts for their neckes, fayr and close joined taches, to arm to mid-thigh; as for the pouldron [shoulder armour] or the vantbrace [arm protection], they may be spared, because they are cumbersome. All this armour is to be rather of russet, sanguine, or blacke colour, than white or milled, for it will keep the longer from rust.'

'These shall have strong, straight, yet nimble pikes of ash-wood, well headed with steel, and armed with plates downward from the head, at least four foote, and the full size or length of every pike shalbe fifteene foote besides the head.

'These pikemen shall also have good, sharpe, and broade swords (of which Turkie and Bilboe are best), strong scabbards chapt with iron, girdle, hangers or bautricke of strong leather; and lastly, if to the pikeman's head peece be fastened a small ring of iron, and to the right side of his back peece (below his girdle) an iron hooke, to hang his steele cap upon, it will be a great ease to the souldier, and a nimble carriage in the time of long marches.'

The use of body armour declined as the war went on, and by 1645 a pikeman was more likely to be wearing a protective coat or cassock, as it was known. For his Irish expedition of 1649 Cromwell ordered 15,000 of these garments coloured Venice Red (the first of the red coats that would become British uniform) and shrunk in water, together with breeches in grey. The wearing of the brimmed and crested metal helmet, the morion, also decreased as the pikemen adopted the wide-brimmed felt hat worn by musketeers. In the New Model Army it appears that there was little, if any, difference in clothing between the two classes of foot soldier.

The introduction of firearms demanded the development of new skills which varied from weapon to weapon. The majority of foot would use matchlock weapons; muskets set off by bringing the glowing end of a chemical-impregnated cord, the

An officer of pikemen, from Grose's Military Antiquities. *He is equipped much as described by Markham.*

match, into contact with gunpowder in a pan to ignite the charge in the barrel of the weapon. More sophisticated methods of firing were in use, but they were expensive and difficult to manufacture and thus employed by the richer combatant, the cavalryman. Edward Davies, published in 1619, wrote of the musketeer:

'If he bear a peece [gun], then must he first learn to hold the same, to accomodate his match betweene his two foremost fingers and his thombe, and to plant the great end [butt] upon his breast with a gallant and souldier-like grace ... His flaske and touch box must keep his powder, his purse and mouth his bullets; in skirmish his left hand must hold his match and peece, and the right hand use the office of charging and discharging.

'In time of marching and travelling by the way, let him keepe a paper in his panne and tuch-hole, and in wet weather have a case for his peece, somewhat portable, or else of necessitie he must keepe the same from wet under his arm-hole or cassocke, or by some other invention free from damage of the weather, and his match in his pocket, onely that except which he burnes: and that likewise so close in the hollow of his hand, or some artificial pipe of pewter hanging at his girdle, as the coale by wet or water go not out...'

A musketeer with match alight in his left hand and his rest in his right. By the time of Naseby the musket itself was often a lighter weapon which made the rest unneccessary.

Davies also discusses the weapon in use and the speed with which it can be reloaded, rejecting the use made by the soldiers of the Low Countries, whom he calls Wallownes, of the bandoleer with containers of powder pre-measured to give the correct charge for loading. They became the norm by the time of the Civil War, with a flask attached for carrying fine power for the priming charge.

[They] 'have used to hang about their neckes, upon a baudricke or border, or at their girdles, certain pipes, which they call charges, of copper and tin, made with covers, which they thinke in skirmish to bee the readie way. But the Spanish dispising that order doth altogether use his flaske. The Frenchman both charge and flaske. But some of our English nation [use] their pocket; which in respect of the danger of the sparks of their match, the uncertaine charge, the expense and spoile of pouder, the discommoditie of wet I account more apt for the show of a triumph and wanton skirmish before ladies and gentlewomen, then fit for the field in a day of service in the face of an enemy:...'

[The musketeer] 'useth a staffe breaste high, in one end a [s]pike to pitch in the ground, and in the other an iron fork to rest his peece upon, and a hoale a little beneath the same in the staffe: whereunto he doth adde a string, which tied and wrapped about his wrist, yeelds him commodity to traine [pull] his fork or staffe after him, whilst he in skirmish doth charge his musket afresh with pouder and bullet.'

At the start of the war most muskets were four foot long and heavy, so a rest was mandatory. From 1643 onwards a shorter, three and a half foot weapon was issued by both sides and a rest was not needed. At Naseby it is likely that both types were present. Rarer and more expensive were snaphaunce or firelock weapons, using flint to strike a spark from steel and thus avoiding the danger, inefficiency and weight inevitably associated with matchlocks. They were issued to artillery guards to reduce the dangers of having lighted matches near powder kegs and some infantry also had them.

The infantry were grouped together in regiments, but numbers were not consistent. The English broadly followed the Dutch, the great innovators in the military arts of the early 17th century, in organizing the pikemen and musketeers in companies of, by 1640, about equal numbers, approximately sixty of each, plus officers, drummers and other ancillaries. There were usually about ten companies to a regiment. However, as the war went on the deviation from the norm became extreme and one of the difficulties of estimating rival strengths flows from the fact that a listing of regiments in an action is a very poor indicator of the number of troops engaged.

The control of a block of more than five dozen pikemen with their long weapons and the efficient deployment of the firepower of a like number of clumsy muskets with gunpowder and glowing match in concert with the pikemen was no mean task. The pikes were used to create a fearsome hedge of spikes for use against other pikemen (at push of pike – a technical phrase for an activity that, in practice, is all too clear) or cavalry and worked well if everyone kept close together. The musketeers had to take turns to discharge to allow their fellows to reload in time to maintain a steady fire. Precise and intense drill had to be undertaken to inculcate the skills and discipline needed to succeed, and it was in part the mistaken idea that the New Model Army would not have been able to do this that led to the Royalist underestimation of their adversaries.

The first stage in the training process was the handling of the weapon. Jacob de Gheyn's drill book was published in 1607 and the illustrations were copied in numerous subsequent manuals. Those reproduced here are from Grose's *Military Antiquities* with his attributions and are typical of the training to which men of both sides were subject in the Civil War. The sequence for pikemen is illustrated with thirty-two pictures in de Gheyn, including shouldering the pike, charging (that is, attacking an enemy with it) and turning about to do the same to the rear, trailing it and making use of both pike and sword. Evidently the whole sequence was yet longer and Colonel William Barriffe in his *Military Discipline or the Young Artillery-man* of 1661 expressly rejects any idea of reducing the number of postures of the pike comprising the drill, explaining the circumstance in which each posture is to be used in battle. The sequence for musketeers is illustrated with over forty drawings covering the loading and firing of the piece twice. There was no formal drill for close-quarter combat when musketeers reversed their weapons and used them as clubs. The demands of fighting with these weapons were clearly daunting.

The manuals then gave numerous exercises to pull these men together into a manoeuverable body. The basic unit was the file, a row of men back to belly and in the English service usually eight men deep. The files were gathered into groups of pikemen eight ranks wide or musketeers four ranks wide and drilled in the five basic aspects: distances, facings, doublings, countermarches and wheelings. Distances governed the space between the men, close order being one foot and a half between both rank and file, according to Barriffe, order three foot, open order six foot and double distance twelve foot. Grose recounts that:

The 3 motion being Shouldered.

Port your Pike in 3 motions.
The 1st motion.

The 2 motion.

The 3 motion being Ported.

Charge your Pike.

Advance your Pike.

Shoulder your Pike in 3 motions.
The 1st motion.

The 2 motion.

The 3 motion being Shouldered.

K.C.Goodnight

PIKE EXERCISE Pl.2.

From the sequence of drills for pikemen.

Diagrams 37 to 42 from musketeers' exercises, which Grose says are from Hogarth, engraved for Mr Blackwell's Account of the Artillery Company.

'The distances of files were regulated by the following rule: for open order, a distance of six feet was taken by each file, standing so far from their right and left hand men, that their arms being mutually extended, their finger ends would just meet. For order, the soldiers putting their hands on their hip bones, with their arms (as the term is) set a-kimbow, the elbows just met or touched those of their right or left hand men. Close order was commanded by the word close; it was one foot and a half distance between the files, and three feet between the ranks; it was for pikes only, and was never to be used but in standing to receive the charge of an enemy; musketeers were never to be closer than the second distance, or order, three feet square, that they might have free use of their arms.'

On this Barriffe disagrees, allowing musketeers close order and in having equal distances between rank and file. These measurements are of importance not only in visualizing how the men fought, but also in working out possible frontages in order to relate alleged numbers of men to possible positions in the field. Barriffe, for example, shows a diagram of a company formed up with a block of eight files of pikemen eight deep with four files, eight deep, of musketeers on each flank and appears to regard this as normal. In practice the actual number of men available and forming the company probably did not conform to the drill book ideal and the commander would have to improvise as best he could.

In addition to verbal commands, orders were given by drumbeat which had some chance of penetrating the din of battle. Barriffe declares that six beats must be learned: a **call**, a **troop**, a **march**, a **preparative**, a **battaile** and a **retreat**. He explains these as follows:

'1: By a **Call**, you must understand to prepare to hear present Proclamation, or else to repaire to your Ensign.

2: By a **Troop**, understand to shoulder your Musket, to advance your Pike, to close your Ranks & Files to their Order, and to Troop along with (or follow) your Officer to the place of *Randezvous*, or elsewhere.

3: By a **March** you are to understand to take your open order in rank, to shoulder both *Mauskets* and Pikes, and to direct your March either quicker or slower, according to the beat of the drum.

4: By a **Preparative** you are to understand to close to your due distance for skirmish both in rank and file, and to make ready, that so you may execute upon the first command.

5: By the **Battail** or charge understand the continuation or pressing forward in order of battaile without lagging behind, rather boldly stepping forward in the place of him that falls dead or wounded, before thee.

6: By a **Retreat**, understand an orderly retiring backward, either for relief, for advantage of ground, or for some other political end, as to draw the enemy into some ambushment, or such like. Much more might be written concerning the Drum, but this may suffice for the present.'

The Cavalry

The horse, like the infantry, was changing at this time, in part because of the increasing use of firearms and in part because the expense of traditional equipment was considerable. Markham's *The Souldiers Accidence* of 1625 appeared in 1643 in an edition combined with two later works and it is from this later edition that Grose quotes the passage on cavalry:

'The first and principall troop of horsemen, for the generality, are now called cuirasiers, or pistoliers, and these men ought to be of the best degree, because, the meanest in one of those troops is ever by his place a gentleman, and so esteemed. They have for defensive armes, gorgets, curats, cutases, which some call culets, others the guard de reine, because it armeth the hinder parts, from the waste to the saddle crootch, then pouldrons, vambraces, a lefthand gauntlet, taces, cuisses, a caske, a sword, girdle and hangers. For offensive armes, they shall have a case of long pistols, firelocks (if it may be), but snaphaunces where they are wanting; the barrels of the pistols would be twenty-six inches long, and the bore of thirty-six bullets in the pound, flask, priming box, key and mouldes ...'

The `lobster-pot' helmet was in common use by cavalry by 1645. The face-guard and peak were hinged so that they could be lifted away from the face.

A common cavalry pistol was the wheellock which was operated by winding up a spring which, when released by the trigger, caused a wheel to strike sparks off a piece of iron pyrites into the pan. It was a fragile machine and expensive to make, and was eventually superseded by flintlock mechanisms. There

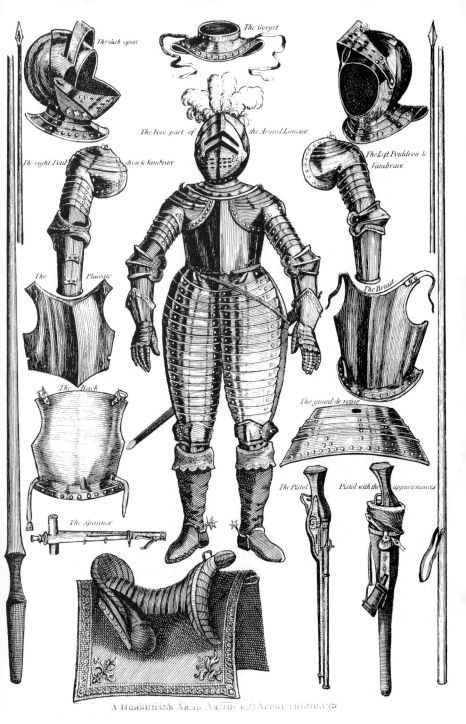

The Casque open

The Gorget

The Fore part of the Armed Lancier

The right Pouldron & Vambrace

The Left Pouldron & Vambrace

The Placcate

The Breast

The Back

The guard de reine

The Pistol

Pistol with the appurtenances

The Spanner

A HORSEMAN'S ARMS, ARMOUR & APPOINTMENTS

A horseman's arms, armour and accoutrements as shown by Grose. This degree
of elaboration was abandoned early in the war.

were a few regiments of cuirassiers fighting in the war, most memorably Sir Arthur Hesilrige's regiment on the Parliamentarian side, which was know as Hesilrige's Lobsters. The close helmet shown in the illustration was by this time giving place to the pot, the familiar lobster-tailed pot with side-pieces or cheeks and a barred, open face protection.

Markham then described the 'hargobusiers or carbines' who were armed with firearms three foot three inches in length and of bore of twenty bullets to the pound of lead, that is, a twenty-bore. The use of the haquebusier as they are more commonly called had ceased by this time, but the third type of horse soldier, the dragoon, was an essential element of the army.

'The last sort of which our horse troops are composed are called dragoons, which are a kind of footmen on horsebacke, and now do succeed the light horsemen, and are of singular use in all actions of warre; their armes defensive, are an open head-piece with cheeks, and a good buffe coat, with deep skirts; and for offensive armes, they have a fair dragon, fitted with an iron

An early type of dragoon or mounted infantryman.

worke to be caryed in a belt of leather, which is buckled over the right shoulder, and under the left arme, having a turnill of iron with a ring, through which the piece runnes up and downe; and these dragons are short pieces of sixteen inches the barrell, and full musket bore [twelve-bore] with firelocks or snaphaunces ... These dragoons in their marches are allowed to be eleven in a rank or file, because when they serve, it is many times on foote, for the maintenance or suprizing of strait [narrow] wayes, bridges or fords, so that when ten men alight to serve, the eleventh holdeth their horses ...'

The 'dragon' was soon superseded by the musket, or by the shorter carbine, with a snaphaunce action. The snaphaunce was an early type of flintlock, much superior to the matchlock which was scarcely a practical weapon for a mounted man. The buff coat was a leather garment developed from the arming doublet worn under body armour to make it comfortable, or at least tolerable, to go about in. Buff coats were increasingly worn by cavalry of all kinds. Markham's suggestion that one man could hold eleven horses in the clamour and turmoil of a fight is marvellously optimistic and must be taken as applicable to peacetime drill. The mounted infantry in the Boer War held about four and the engraving of the Battle of Naseby by Robert Streeter, published in 1647, seems to show groups of five or six horses. The supplement to Barriffe's edition of 1661 was a brief set of instructions for the cavalry by one 'J.B.' and this said of the dragoons when they dismounted for action:

'Being so a-lighted, every one of them is to Cast his Bridle over the neck of his Side-mans Horse in the same Order as they Marched; keeping them so together, by the help of such as are thereunto especially appointed.'

This seems to be a practical way of increasing the number of horses that can be held, but still does not give a clear answer.

The basic operational unit of cavalry was described by J.B. as:

'A Troop of Horse of sixty, that (in the beginning of the late Civil War amongst us) having been the usual Number allowed in a Troop, which afterwards were enlarged, or lessened, according as the then Powers did suppose most Convenient, for the carrying on of their Designs.'

A regiment might be made up of as many as ten troops. J.B. then continues to show the troop sub-divided for exercises into three squadrons or divisions composed of seven files three deep; that is, of sixty-three men, of whom three are the corporals added to the sixty troopers. The unit also has a captain, a lieutenant, a cornet, a quarter-master, and two trumpeters shown in the exercise diagrams and a farrier and a saddler, presumably non-combatant as a rule. A six-deep formation was usual when the war began, but by 1645 three deep was normal. The Streeter engraving shows formations with files five deep, but it is not clear whether this is a true report of a formation adopted because of the narrowness of the front or merely an artistic convenience. The instructions on exercising go on:

'Your Troop of Horse, being drawn into the Field, before you
can Exercise them, you must draw up the several Divisions,
into an even Body, in the manner of a Battalia ...'

The arrangement is to place the three squadrons side by side with the captain's on the right, the cornet's in the centre and the quarter-master's on the left with the lieutenant at its rear. The trumpeters are in attendance on the captain. As in the infantry, open order is defined ('four foot between file and file, whereby a horse may march up between') and close order can be understood when the doubling of the front rank is achieved by having it initially at open order and then doubled by the rear rank passing throught the middle one to fill the spaces in the front rank. The four foot space would be filled entirely by this maneouvre, creating a cuisse to cuisse (thigh to thigh) or knee to knee formation.

The extent to which the pistol was used in preference to the sword is significant when trying to reconstruct action from the evidence of pistol balls discovered on the battlefield. The cavalry was not used to charge blocks of pikemen who presented a hedgehog-like obstacle and in theory the carbine or pistol was to be discharged at them. Elaborate diagrams show how the horseman advances, fires his weapon and retires to reload. Not, in practice, very credible as the almost stationary assailant would be a ready target for the pikeman's attendant musketeers. At Naseby cavalry fought cavalry, only attacking infantry either at its peril or when disorder rendered foot soldiers vulnerable. The Dutch, whom the Parliamentarians emulated, favoured the use of firearms first and then the charge at a good trot, but the Royalists preferred to get their charge in as quickly as possible in the Swedish manner. In his summary of 1661, enlightened by wartime experience, J.B. says:

[The soldier] 'is to take notice, that he is not to discharge his
Pistoll, till he comes to his Enemies Horses head, or rather to
keep his Pistolls for a Reserve, and Charge his Enemy with the
Swords point, and so to endeavour to Charge throw [through]

Plate XXXIX from Grose. His captions read: a buff coat, sword, shoulder-belt, toledo, and a defence for the left arm, worn in the time of Charles I by Sir Francis Rhodes, Bart. of Balborough Hall, Derbyshire. He explains that the belt has a loop and swivel to carry a carbine. The sword belt is also buff and the weapon is two feet five inches long and belonged to a suit of common iron armour, with a barred helmet, of which the cuirass had rusted away. The weapon on the right is the toledo with a blade of three feet nine inches.

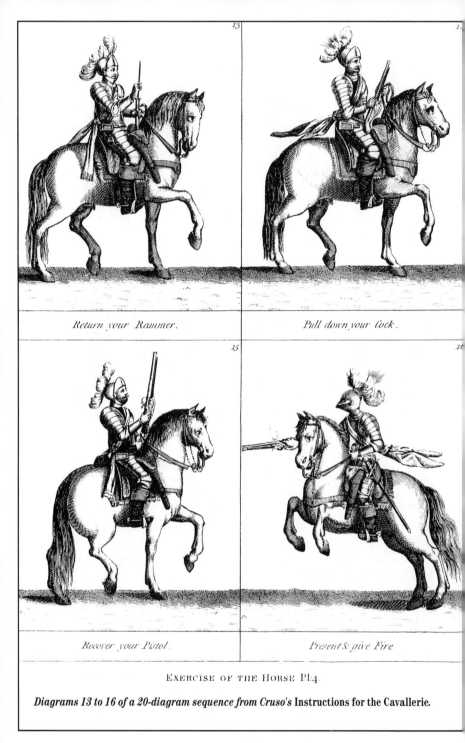

Return your Rammer.

Pull down your Cock.

Recover your Pistol.

Present & give Fire

EXERCISE OF THE HORSE Pl.4.

Diagrams 13 to 16 of a 20-diagram sequence from Cruso's **Instructions for the Cavallerie.**

and Break his Enemies Body [formation], and then his Pistolls
will be of use in a Pursuite.'
This point is supported by the observation on the possible frequency
of use of the pistol. J.B. declares that the six or eight charges for the
pistol held by the spanner, which is used with the cavalry wheellock
pistol, are sufficient as:

'it having been rarely known, that in any Battel, the Cavalry
have had occasion to Fire their Pistolls so often as to spend so
much powder. Nevertheless it is requisite that the Shouldier
have a small powder horn full of good powder, in his Pocket, for
a Reserve.'

The Train and the Baggage

Artillery did not play a significant part in the Battle of Naseby, but
both sides had guns with them. Some authorities say the Royalists
had twelve guns, others say twenty; a mix of field and siege pieces.
Streeter's engraving of the battalia shows eight Parliamentary guns.
The movement of these weapons required carts and wagons to carry
shot and powder and the men to work the ordnance. Peter Young,
who favoured the dozen gun Royalist train, lists thirty-four gunners
and twice that of assistant gunners or matrosses, twenty pioneers and
thirty-three carters as well as thirty-five other people, thirty-three
carts and nearly 250 horses. Glenn Foard suggests that the artillery
train alone would need at least fifteen wagons or carts and seventy-
five horses. To these must be added wagons for the carriage of
match, powder and shot for the handguns, provisions, tents and other
necessaries, bringing the total needed to forty. Further, the army
trailed behind it a cloud of followers, wives and women who were not
wives. On the Parliamentarian side Streeter shows the baggage
laager with about twenty wagons in it, clearly insufficient for the
support of Fairfax's forces, and yet another reason to treat this
pictorial evidence with caution. The need for good roads for the
reliable progress of such trains needs no emphasis, and the
practicality of movement over muddy terrain and across the
numerous rivers was a principal consideration for military men.

The Terrain

Northamptonshire straddles the key routes from London to the
north. In the east the Great North Road, now the A1, passes
Peterborough beyond which lay the marshes of the Fens, where

Cornelius Vermuyden had yet to complete his work of drainage. In the centre another Roman Road, Watling Street, now the A5, was still a major route, though the main road veered westwards at Weedon Bec to pass Daventry and then branch towards Coventry or to give access to Warwick and the Vale of Evesham. John Ogilby's *Britannia*, a route guide showing roads as if on a continuous scroll, was published in 1675. The same way of showing roads is used for motorways in modern road atlases. Ogilby marks the continuation of Watling Street north of Weedon as 'the Street way to Watford gap'. At Daventry he shows three turnings to the right from the Coventry road, to Leicester and Lutterworth, to Northampton and London Bridge and to Dodford. The presence of this last, to Dodford, makes it clear that the modern route to Northampton through Flore did not yet exist. Daventry thus dominated both the routes from the south to Coventry and also the route from the north towards Banbury and Oxford; the road being taken by Charles I when the Battle of Cropredy Bridge took place in 1644. In medieval times the development of commerce and the trend to central government required improved communications and the building and maintenance of bridges was essential. John Speed's map of Northamptonshire, published as late as 1610, shows no roads but does mark some of the bridges and gives impressive coverage of the river systems. Roads were added to an up-date of the earliest topographical mapping of England, that of Christopher Saxton, made by Philip Lea in about 1690, but these were evidently major through-routes and lesser roads were omitted. Maps are discussed in greater detail below.

From Speed's map and the modern diagram of the rivers and their medieval bridges, the constraints on the movement of an army with an artillery and baggage train can be understood. The roads themselves were poor and in wet weather soon became quagmires. The Highways Act of 1555 had put the burden of road maintenance on the parishes through which they passed but failed to grant them the revenue to fund the work. The next development did not take place until 1663 when part of the Great North Road was made a toll road, but at the time of the Civil War Northamptonshire had few roads worthy of the name and those were rough. Most of the routes were unsuitable for wheeled vehicles in wet weather, and the summer of 1645 was unusually wet. Indeed, some forty years later Lady Celia Fiennes wrote of her journey from Warwick to Northampton on what

A detail from Speed's map of 1610, indicative of the mapping available to the commanders of the campaign in Northamptonshire in June 1645. Rivers and some of the bridges are shown, hilly areas are suggested but not precisely located and roads are omitted entirely.

HASELWOOD COLLECTION.

was still a principal route:

> 'From Warwick we went towards Daventry all along part of the Vale of the Red Horse which was very heavy way and could not reach thither being 14 mile; about 11 mile we came to a place called Nether Shugar [Shuckburgh] a sad village, we could have no entertainment [find nowhere to stay]; just by it on a steep hill is Shuggbery Hall a seate of Sir Charles Shuggberrys [Shuckburgh] who seeing our distress, being just night and the horses weary with the heavy way, he very curteously tooke compassion on us ...'

From the river system diagram an understanding of the terrain can be developed. The basin of the River Nene, which runs through Northampton and Oundle towards Peterborough and the sea at the Wash, occupies most of the county. The river's headwaters are to the south of Daventry with a major tributary coming to Northampton from the north and another, the Ise and the Slade, emanating from a

THE RIVER SYSTEMS OF NORTHAMPTONSHIRE

The crosses indicate the sites of Medieval bridges

NORTHAMPTONSHIRE
RECORD SOCIETY

point yet further north, running east and then turning south. From much the same northern place the River Welland sets off north-west briefly before turning eastwards through Market Harborough on its way to the Wash. On the western flank of the county the River Cherwell flows to Oxford and the Thames while, in the north, the River Avon sets off for Warwick, Stratford, the Severn valley and the Bristol Channel. The Ise, Welland and Avon all have their origins in the high land on which the villages of Naseby and Sibbertoft are situated. Indeed, the Reverend John Mastin, Vicar of Naseby, when writing his history of the village in 1792 claimed that it was the highest place in England. While he is mistaken, to stand outside the village on the Thornby road and have a clear sight of the old testing tower of the Northampton Lift Company on the outskirts of the town almost persuades you that he was correct.

From Northampton roads fanned out much as they do today to the west and the north. What is now the A45 to Flore, Weedon and Daventry was not a main road, but more of a track for pedestrians and horse-riding folk. At Flore it seems probable that it took a direct line to Dodford, maybe across a ford, and continued to Daventry. A more important route was by Nobottle to Whilton Lodge, the old Roman road from Duston to Bannaventa (reputedly the birthplace of St Patrick) on Watling Street and so to Daventry. There was a bridge at Whilton and another a couple of miles south at Brockhall. Through Harlestone and East and West Haddon a major road followed much the same route as the modern A428. The equally major road northwards from Northampton went, as it does today, to a fork at Kingsthorpe where the Spratton-Welford-Leicester road (A5199) ran on the west side of the basin of the Northern Water draining into the Nene while the direct route to Market Harborough (now A508) crossed the medieval bridges at Pitsford and Great Oxendon on its way.

Lateral routes that were more than tracks between villages are harder to define with confidence. There is evidence that the road from Kelmarsh, on the Market Harborough road, westwards to Naseby was suitable for wheeled vehicles and, after the valley had been negotiated, it probably continued through Cold Ashby towards West Haddon or Long Buckby. Ogilby marks the turning at Kelmarsh as being for Coventry but the low land west of Naseby must, in wet weather, have been muddy and difficult.

Today the drainage of the area east of Watling Street has been transformed by the building of the Grand Union Canal and the reservoirs made to supply it with water. Add to this the drainage encouraged by expanding arable farming and it takes a leap of imagination to visualize what the land was like in 1645, but make that leap we must if we seek understanding. This countryside was of strategic importance because of its through-routes and it also presented tactical difficulties to both sides in the manouevres leading up to the battle.

Maps

Both armies depended a great deal on local knowledge and on scouting. Useful maps were not available, for of those that existed Speed was the very latest thing. There was good representation of rivers and reasonable accuracy in positioning towns, but hills were merely sketched. The bridges were correctly positioned but not all of them were shown. Roads were missing entirely.

The first modern topographical survey of England and Wales was undertaken by Christopher Saxton who began in 1573 and produced thirty-four county maps between 1574 and 1579 and a complete map in 1583. His map including Northamptonshire was made in 1576 and was overtaken by Speed's in 1610, about the time of Saxton's death. Engraved map plates were valuable assets and Saxton's plates were bought, improved and also copied by others who replaced his name with their own. The outbreak of war stimulated a new wave of publications, but still without roads and lacking useful representation of terrain, other than rivers.

Henry Hexham translated the text for the English edition of the Mercator-Hondius-Janssonius Atlas of 1636. He was not insensible to the importance of maps for military purposes, describing himself on the title page as Quartermaster to the Regiment of Colonel Goring. He wrote:

'what Generall is there, which conducts his Armie through passages, over Rivers, Brookes, Mountaines or Woods, quarter or lodge them, or beseige any Citty, Towne or fort, but he maust have continually a Topographick description, and Map of that Countrie, towne or place in his hand, to advance his intended designe.'

The sentiment is apt. The actuality of available maps fell far short.

The main use of maps was as an adjunct to newspaper reports of the war and as tools for military support services. In 1644 Thomas Jenner, a printmaker supporting the Parliamentarian cause, produced

Lea's revised version of Saxton's map. The dotted lines are the boundaries between the hundreds into which the county was divided. The roads are shown as twin lines of dashes from Northampton to Market Harborough (due north), to Coventry (north-west) and to Stoney Stratford (due south). The Holy Head (north Wales) road is shown as continuous twin lines passing through Daventry. BODLEIAN LIBRARY C17:46

a revised version of Saxton's wall map in a form known subsequently as the Quartermaster's Map. It was advertised as:

'Usefull for all Comanders for Quarteringe of Souldiers, & all sorts of Persons, that would be informed, Where the Armies be; neuer so Commodiously drawne before this, 1644. Described by one that trauailed [travelled] throughout the whole kingdome, for its purpose. Sold by Thomas Ienner at the South entrance of ye Exchange, W:Hollar fecit.'

The military application was thus seen as limited to the solution of the billeting problem, and as this included forage for horses on a very considerable scale as well as the need to feed off the land, it was of no small importance. But the map was not much use for planning attacks or defence, nor was it meant to be. Saxton's county maps had come into the hands of an Oxford bookseller, William Web, and he revised them and issued them as an atlas at some time in 1645.

Saxton's plates were acquired from William Morgan, successor to Ogilby, by Philip Lea in the 1680s. A catalogue of his, published some twenty years later, gives details of his improvements to Saxton's works.

'The Original Map of England and Wales, with all the small Towns, Villages, Private Seats of the King, Nobility and Gentry, Roads and cross Roads, from Town to Town, by Inspection, in 20 sheets, ... price 15s.'

It is interesting to see which roads in Northamptonshire are of sufficient importance to warrant inclusion on Lea's map, for they give a fair indication of which roads were generally suitable for wheeled traffic.

The two sides were thus, at the start of the 1645 campaign season, very much equal in most respects. The outcome would depend on the quality of their leadership.

The equipment and armour of a Parliamentarian officer of the new Model Army. ROYAL ARMOURIES LEEDS

Chapter 2

TO FIGHT OR NOT TO FIGHT – 1 MAY TO 13 JUNE 1645

In the spring of 1645 Parliament appeared to have the upper hand in terms of territorial control having secured the north of England and acquired the aid of the Scots. The Royalists, however, had cause for optimism because the massive reorganization of their enemies in creating the New Model Army was incomplete. Both sides suffered from a lack of strategic vision in the highest level of their command.

The Royalist Plan

In the west country the Royalists, under the command of Lord Goring, were besieging the major Parliamentarian garrison at Taunton which they expected to take within the month. In the Welsh Marches Prince Rupert was planning to raise more men from the south-west to retake the lost territory in the north. In Oxford the King was preparing his army for the field, but though he was well-supplied with infantry and artillery, he lacked cavalry, and Cromwell was raiding in the locality to keep the King bottled up in the town. In his History of the Great Rebellion the Earl of Clarendon describes the attempt to create a plan of action.

'... on the last day of April ... General Goring was sent for by the king to draw his horse and dragoons towards Oxford, that thereby his majesty might free himself from Cromwell, who, with a very strong party of horse and dragoons, lay in wait to interrupt his joining with Price Rupert about Worcester. How unwelcome soever these orders were to Lord Goring, yet there was no remedy but he must obey them: and it was now hoped that the west should be hereafter freed from him, where he was at that time very ungracious.

Fortunately Goring caught part of the Parliamentarian force at a crossing of the Isis (Thames) River and put them to flight, thus arriving for his meeting with his king at Woodstock on 7 May covered in glory.

Meanwhile Prince Rupert and Prince Maurice were coming east with their forces and part of Goring's while the King had left Oxford with an artillery train of fourteen guns, his lifeguard of horse and his infantry. The journey to the eventual council of war at Stow on the Wold was dogged by harrassing attacks by their enemies, but no significant loss was suffered. Clarendon remarked:

'The next day after Goring came to the king, the army was drawn to a rendezvous, and consisted then of five thousand foot and above six thousand horse. If it had been kept together, it is very probable that the summer might have been crowned with better success.'

King Charles leaving Oxford during the campaign.

Two possible plans were proposed. Goring advocated making for Taunton in order to force Fairfax to come to battle with his untried New Model Army while it yet lacked sufficient cavalry. Rupert proposed marching first to relive Chester, then Pontefract and thence to retake the north country. On 10 May the king gave the orders that split his forces in two, releasing Goring to go west with an independent command while himself, with Rupert, setting off for Chester. On their way to Worcester, they passed through Evesham, where they were joined by Sir Jacob Astley with over 3,000 foot, unaware that this line of communication would soon be lost to them. Then, on 20 May, they were met by Lord Byron at Market Drayton. He brought the news that their approach had caused the siege of Chester to be lifted. The king turned east, presumably to head eventually for Pontefract, but by 26 May, when at Burton on Trent, heard that Fairfax had merely made a feint towards Taunton and was, in fact, investing Oxford, Charles's capital. The northern expedition could not be continued.

The Parliamentarian Plan

Decisiveness and clarity of thought was lacking on the Parliamentarian side as well. The war was being prosecuted by the

Committee for Both Kingdoms, an Anglo-Scottish affair to which General Fairfax reported. It also issued orders direct to Cromwell, who, in spite of being a Member of Parliament, was continued in command of the cavalry. He was sent in pursuit of the king while Fairfax was told to besiege Oxford, and part of the cavalry under Colonel Vermuyden (Cornelius's son) was sent off north to join the Scots. Parliament, too, had divided their army until such time as the Royalist intentions became clear. On 17 May Cromwell was directed to support Fairfax and by 22 May they were at Marston commencing siege works, but without Parliament having furnished the necessary supplies and munitions. It was clearly a futile undertaking. The Committee, meanwhile, was without any plan to engage Charles in battle, but was sending small bodies of troops here and there in a frenzy of petty activity based on the guess that he was still heading north. Then the possibility that the Eastern Association might be the Royalist target led them to issue a new order to Cromwell on 26 May; he was to return to Ely, Vermuyden was to come south again and a jigsaw of consequential troops movements was to ensue.

The Taking of Leicester

Rupert had already sent for Goring to bring both horse and foot to reinforce the king and, as they were all confident that Oxford could hold out, the Royalists decided to strike at a Parliamentarian garrison in order to draw Fairfax off. The lot fell on Leicester. Clarendon wrote:

> 'They had no considerable town so near the place where the king then was as Leicester, in which there was a good garrison. Prince Rupert (who was always well pleased with any brisk attempt) cheerfully entertained the first motion, and sent Sir Marmaduke Langdale forthwith to surround it (which was of great extent) with his [Northern] horse.'

Although considered poorly fortified, Leicester's medieval defences had been strengthened with earthworks and wooden palisades. On 30 May the siege began and the garrison was invited to surrender. As there was no response cannon were brought to bear on the stone walls of the Newark, a walled area next to the castle, and by evening a breach had been made. The assault that night was a hard, bloody affair. Three attempts were made to break into Newark and each was repulsed. The attacks on the north and east of the town did better but once within the place the Royalists found themselves in a bitter street battle, under fire from the house windows by men they could not see.

The stories of atrocities committed in revenge for this resistance were many and extreme. Most certainly the town was comprehensively plundered. Casualty reports vary widely, and may have been as high as 300 Parliamentarian and 400 Royalist dead, and 300 defenders taken prisoner.

The effect on morale was marked. Not only had the king's men scored a notable feat of arms, they had also acquired substantial booty. Further, they were viewed as a very real threat by their enemies, for only Rockingham stood between them and the previously secure territory of the Association in East Anglia. There was, of course, blame to be apportioned and the Committee for Both Kingdoms collected, rightly, a great deal of it. The Independents in Parliament took every advantage of the Committee's discomfiture and forced the issue. On 9 June the Committee agreed to devolve command on Fairfax entirely and also, after a debate in the Commons on 10 June, to permit him to appoint Cromwell his Lieutenant General of Horse. The Royalist success at Leicester and their plundering of Northamptonshire afterwards helped to fashion the power that would bring about their downfall.

The Dawdle to Daventry

The success at Leicester had not solved Oxford's problem, for the fall of Evesham cut lines of communication to Royalist terrritory in the River Severn valley so that only well-guarded convoys could bring supplies to the city. Other options were open. The king could retake control in the West Midlands or even revert to the scheme of going north, but in the end the relief of Oxford was fixed upon. Clarendon observed:

'Leicester was a post where the king might, with all possible convenience and honour, have sat still till his army might have been recruited [strengthened], as well as thoroughly refreshed. Colonel Gerard was upon his march towards him from Wales, with a body of three thousand horse and foot: he had reason to expect that Lord Goring would be very shortly with him with his horse ... the king saw cause to repent his separation, and sent other orders to recall him as soon as was possible. But the king's fate, and the natural unsteadiness and irresolution of those about him, hurried him into counsels very disagreeable to the posture he was in. He knew not that Fairfax was gone from Oxford ... the king resolved to march directly for Oxford ...'

Sir Henry Slingsby recorded in his diary his understanding of the news:

> 'Here came also ye news to ye King of taking Evesham & ye Sr. Tho. Fairfax had beseig'd Oxford & likewise some intimation from thence, yt ye town was not so well provid'd for a seige; wch stopt ye King in his march & turn'd his thoughts how to relieve it. It was no little trouble to our Northern men to think upon marching Southward again, & began to hang backward, & discover their discontent ...'

The grumbling men of the Northern Horse were eventually persuaded to stay with the king and, on 5 June, they marched to Market Harborough. Meanwhile small parties of Royalist horse raided the countryside, carrying off cattle and other supplies.

To the Parliamentarians this had the appearance of an advance on Northampton or Rockingham. Sir John Norwich, Governor of Rockingham Castle, wrote:

> 'I expect them before me ere morning. We shall not be wanting to entertain them according to the utmost of our abilities, being recruited by the addition of some horse and foot ...'

That same day some 200 horse were reported facing Northampton where Colonel Whetham's men sallied forth to attack them and were said to have captured some of them.

The advance of the main body continued on 7 June. Sir Edward Walker recorded:

> '... Next Day at Harborow had News that Fairfax was drawn off from Oxford, without having made any Attempt or Approach, and without doing or suffering much; and that after he had likewise attempted Bostal [Boarstall] House, where he was notably repulsed by Sir William Campion the Governour, with some Loss, that he was marched towards Buckingham. This was not welcome News, yet such as obliged us rather to make towards him and hazard a Battel, than to march Northwards and be met in the Face with the Scots, and have him in our Rear. From Harborow the Army marched to Daventry ...'

Sir Samuel Luke, governor of the Parliamentarian garrison at Newport Pagnell, states that the rendezvous for the Royalists forces on 7 June was at Cold Ashby and the heavy wagons left Market Harborough over the medieval bridge across the Welland on the Kelmarsh road, the main road for Northampton, before turning west, possibly up the ridge road into Naseby. That there was a need to declare a rendezvous makes it clear that more than one route was used; not everyone started from the same place. Men and horses were quartered in villages all about the town in order to have water and forage, and so would make their way by the most convenient route to Cold Ashby and thence to Daventry. Edward Fitzgerald, whose family owned a great part of Naseby in the early 19th Century, corresponded with Thomas Carlyle about the battle and wrote to him on 30 September 1842 reporting stories about an army having passed through Cold Ashby and remarked:

'I should therefore suppose that it was more probably the Royalist than the Parliament army, since Cold Ashby certainly lies between Borough Hill and Naseby. One story indeed yet extant at Cold Ashby tells of both armies: that the Royalists were busy eating the good man's bacon at the Inn, in his absence: he returned suddenly, and the fellows asked him where the Rebels were: he said, close behind him: on which they decamped and he saved his bacon.'

At Daventry the king lodged at the Wheatsheaf Inn at the south end of Sheaf Street. The building is now an old people's home.

The Royalist army encamped on the Iron Age fort on Borough Hill. The hill is to the east of the town and commands the road from London via Weedon Bec to Coventry as well as the route passing through Kilsby to the north towards Banbury and Oxford. Evidently this has been a key through-route since pre-historic times. Slingsby wrote:

'... ye King at Dantry had sent a Convoy to Oxford, & stays their return. In this Interim Sr. Tho. Fairfax was come about with his army to Northampton, & some of his horse in our Quarters, before we were aware of ym. This made ye King draw his whole army together & take ye Hills yt were about Dantry, yt wch is called Daws [Danes] Hills; where yet one may see ye intrenchments of an army, & so high as it overlooks a good part of ye Country between it & Northampton; & there upon yt Hill ye whole army of Horse & foot stood in arms yt same night.'

This report runs events together, for it was not until the night of 12 to 13 June that they took alarm at the closeness of the New Model Army.

The Approach of Fairfax

When he learned that the king's men were near Northampton on 6 June, Fairfax decided not to make for Buckingham but for Great

The ramparts of the ancient fort on Borough Hill, Daventry, are part-hidden with patches of impenetrable gorse or furze, giving an idea of how great an impediment such vegetation was at Naseby. Even on a misty day, as here, the hill commands good views to Weedon over the 17th century route to Coventry and to the old Roman Watling Street running north.

Brickhill and on to Newport Pagnell which he reached on 7 June. Here the Governor was not best pleased to see him, for he, a good Presbyterian, regarded the New Model as being a gang of rascally Independents. Indeed, the religious differences undermined the coherence of the army. Sir Samuel Luke wrote in a letter of, perhaps, 12 June:

'Col. Vermuyden has left his charge and would have taken leave of the General but he dare not dismiss him till he has liberty from Parliament ... I hear several officers have petitioned that General that they may have liberty to leave the army, they being not able to live with that ungodly crew. They are grown so wild since they came near the enemy that our devout Christians cannot abide them ... Sir T Fairfax had intelligence from his Scoutmaster that all his Majesty's forces in Winchester, Basing, Faringdon, Oxford, Boarstall and Wallingford were drawn out to come to his assistance at Daventry, which was nothing but a scarecrow. It is true they were all drawn together but it was only to convoy the plunder which his Majesty sent to Oxford...

The reliability of Luke's observations can be measured by his misunderstanding of the Royalist strength, for it is known that the

43

Musketeers on the march. ECWS

reinforcements he speaks of were not forthcoming.

Joshua Sprigge sheds rather more light on the New Model Army's march.

> 'The next day, June 7, the Army marched to Sherrington, a mile East of Newport-Pagnel, to the end the forces with Colonel Vermuden ... might more conveniently joyn, but especially to be on that side of the River, the better to secure the Association, in case the King, who the day before had faced Northampton, and seemed to intend that way, should attempt to break into it ...

> 'Lords day, June 8. the Army resting in their quarters, severall parties of horse were sent out as far as Tocester, to gain intelligence of the motions of the Kings Army, who brought in some prisoners ...'

The probing by both sides went on. Luke wrote on Wednesday 11 June:

> 'A party of firelocks came into Whittlewood Forest this day, which took some of Sir T. Fairfax's stragglers. A party of 2 or 300 horse of his Majesty's early this morning plundered Towcester and all of the towns thereabouts, committing some cruelties in Chipping [Green's?] Norton. This afternoon some 700 horse and foot came to Towcester which they reported intended to quarter there ...'

It may be that Luke is not entirely accurate, but the accumulation of reports does suggest that the opposing sides were in contact quite early in the week. There is also a report of a trumpeter, the usual messenger between armies at this time, coming in to the Royalist camp on Tuesday 10 June to discuss an exchange of prisoners. If, therefore, Prince Rupert was unaware of the proximity of the Parliamentarians there must have been something seriously wrong within his own army as far as appreciation of intelligence was concerned.

Speed's 1610 plan of Northampton. The south and west were well protected by the river, castle and walls but the curtain wall on the north and east was dangerously weak. After the taking of Leicester, the fall of Northampton was a real possibility. HASELWOOD COLLECTION

It was while Fairfax was at Newport Pagnell that he obtained authorization to retain Cromwell as his Lieutenant General of Horse, as Sprigge commented, 'to the great content of the General, and the whole Army'.

Sprigge's account continues:

'... on Wednesday, June 11, though a rainy day, marched from Stony-Stratford to Wooton, within three miles of Northampton, where intelligence still confirmed the Kings continuance at Daventry ... But afterwards it appeared, that his stay there, was only till a part of 1200 horse were returned, which he sent from his Army to Oxford, as a convoy with the plundered cattel & sheep of Leicestershire, Northamptonshire, &c. the better to enable Oxford to endure a seige ... himself being intent upon a march for the relief of Pomfract [Pontefract] and Scarborough.'

Although Northampton was solid for Parliament it was not equipped to entertain a great army and the supplies at the first campsite, on the ridge at Wooton, two miles to the south, had to be supplemented by the Mayor and magistrates of the town. Accordingly they moved the next day, Thursday 12 June, to Kislingbury on the River Nene to the west. Sprigge erroneously records this place as Guilsborough, but adds:

'... (four miles on the west of Northampton and within five miles of Burrough-hill, where the Enemy still continued).'

So it is clear where he means, although it is only three miles from Northampton and a good seven from Borough Hill. Luke wrote to the Earl of Essex on 13 June saying:

'Our army lies this night at Kislingbury, within 5 miles of Daventry, our horse sentries within pistol shot of each other. His Majesty entrenches himself on the top of Burrough Hill (as they say). The army for numbers of men, horse and arms is the gallantest that I have yet seen in England for stout soldiers and willing men to fight, and if God will do his work by multitudes I am confident it will be done now ...'

Parliamentarian patrols continued to scout towards the Royalist positions to the west. The River Nene runs from the west to Kislingbury and Northampton, and was bridged as early as 1329 at Weedon Bec to carry the London (via Watling Street) to Coventry road. This is shown on Speed's map of 1610, which also labels Weedon, in error, as Roman Bannaventa. Downstream, to the east, another bridge is shown at Heyford. The bridge at Kislingbury is

Speed's map of Northamptonshire with Kislingbury bridge arrowed.

noted in a document of 1540 and also appears on Speed's map. Fairfax, as usual, had kept the river between his force and his enemy. Running southwards to the east of Watling Street to join the Nene at Weedon Bec is a tributary now obscured and redirected by the building of the Grand Union Canal and, at the time, probably meandering through marshy water-meadows. Speed shows this as being bridged at Whilton, the real Bannaventa, where the Roman road from Duston, on the western outskirts of Northampton, crosses to Watling Street. South of that, at Brockhall, Speed shows another bridge of which records from 1392 exist. The modern A45 is misleading as the Flore to Weedon bridge certainly post-dates Eyre's map of 1779. In 1645 there was probably no bridge at all, but a ford on a line between Flore and Dodford that is now a bridleway on the east and a minor road west of Watling Street (A5), and on which a bridge was built when the turnpike road was made, as shown on the Dodford parish map of 1742. From this the guess must be that the Royalists would have guarded the bridges at Whilton and Brockhall with care and placed a picket at Flore or Heyford to give warning of an approach.

If this is correct, the picket was made up of a fairly inattentive bunch of men. Sprigge reports:

[Fairfax's men] 'Marching in very good order; for that they did advance directly upon the place where the enemy had pitcht himself. A commanded party of Horse gave the Enemy an alarm, and took some prisoners, by whom they understood the King was a hunting, the Souldiers in no order, and their horses all at grasse, having not the least knowledge of our advance, and being in the greatest security that could be; but the alarm was so quickly taken thorow all their quarters, that our Foot being somewhat behinde, and night approaching, it was not thought wisdome to make any further attempt.'

This was, presumably, the incident to which Slingsby refers before describing the position at Daventry. As it happened, the Oxford convoy returned that same evening and, as the intention had always been to move north as soon as the resupply of Oxford had been achieved, haste was made to break camp at once.

As Sprigge records, Fairfax himself was abroad on the night of 12/13 June.

'As the General was riding in the morning about three of the clock, within a mile and a half of Flowre, where the Enemy kept an horse-guard; He could discern the Enemy riding fast over Burrough-hill, to make fires in abundance, as if they were firing their Huts; which gave some cause to believe they were about to march ...'

Fairfax returned to Kislingbury but, Sprigge again,

'...having forgot the Word [password], he was stopped at the very first Guard; and requiring the Souldier that stood Sentinel, to give it to him, he refused to do it, telling him he was to demand the Word from all that past him, but to give it to none, and so made the General stand in the wet, till he sent for the Captain of the guard to recieve his commission to give the General the word ...'

At five o'clock in the morning of Friday 13 June Fairfax's scoutmaster, Watson, confirmed that the Royalists were moving off and a Council of War was convened at six. In the middle of the discussion Oliver Cromwell arrived with some 600 horse and dragoons; a blessing indeed. A troop of horse under Major Harrison was sent towards Daventry to keep watch and report back and a fighting patrol under Colonel Ireton was sent further north to grasp any opportunity to attack the Royalist flank. The main body then set off in the direction, so Sprigge says, of Market Harborough.

Exactly what route was followed to Guilsborough is not known. The cavalry and, indeed, the foot could well have gone through Harpole and up the hill in a direct line towards Nobottle, but the artillery and baggage would need to keep to roads. As Sprigge has said, it rained on the march to Wooton and was raining when poor

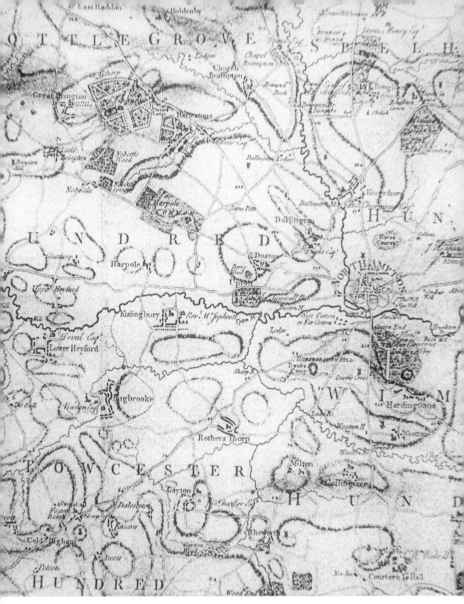

Detail from Thomas Eyre's map of Northamptonshire as revised by William Faden in 1779 and 1791. Possible routes northwards from Kislingbury can be seen passing around the Spencer estate at Althorp. Northampton Record Office 1298

Fairfax forgot the password. Taking wagons cross-country was not an option. Once over the bridge at Kislingbury the obvious route was to turn in the direction of Northampton for a little way before heading north to get onto the Roman road from Duston. Indeed, Foard points

The medieval bridge at Kislingbury from the north bank of the Nene.

out that no compensation was paid to Harpole for crop damage which cutting the corner would have caused, so the whole army may well have been assembled on Harpole Common which lay on the northern side of the Roman road, halfway between Duston and Nobottle. From here they would pass around Althorp, the estate of the Spencer family, then north around East Haddon, Ravensthorpe and Coton to Guilsborough. This route minimizes river fords and holds to high ground as much as possible, a choice open to a force that had held this territory since the start of the war, commanded local loyalties and would thus be well informed about roads. Many of the places on the route lie just to one side of the main road, by-passed, an arrangement typical of established droving roads, for no one wants a great herd of cattle fouling the highway outside the front door.

The Royalist Return to Harborough

Prince Rupert tried to confuse his enemies as to his intentions by sending his advance party off along the Warwick road, but it soon became clear that they were actually heading north, joining Watling Street at Kilsby. Slingsby wrote:

Pikemen on the march. ECWS

'The next Morning were comand'd to march back again to Harborrow, & in our march we understood yt General Fairfax follow'd wth his army upon ye side of us 6 miles distant.'
Having already come from Harborough the Royalists would be aware that the River Avon, rising at Naseby had to be crossed. The direct

Helmet dating from the English Civil War period. Note the adjustable face guard. TAYLOR LIBRARY

route, around the headwaters, by which they had come would expose the flank of their marching body, which Foard calculates as being some six miles long, to an attack by Fairfax's horse. They were quite right; Ireton had been sent off with orders to do just that. It was therefore necessary for at least the diversionary part of the army to undertake the longer, more tiring march to cross the Avon further up Watling Street, perhaps at Catthorpe, and march along the northern bank and then along the Welland valley. Ogilby's *Britannia* has a map of England with his major roads marked as mapped and described in detail in the body of the book. This map also shows some of the lesser roads, marked to tie up with the text labels on turnings off the main roads on the detailed route maps. One of these suggests a bridge crossing the Nene tributary on a road from Watling Street north of Whilton, perhaps on the way to Long Buckby, from which it was, and still is, an easy march to Watford. Another, dotted, line goes north from Daventry, turns east and then north, maybe at Crick and on through Yelvertoft (the scale is such that no village place-names are shown) to cross the River Avon at a place which is possibly Stanford on Avon before turning east for Market Harborough. A possible interpretation is therefore that part of the Royalist army marched

King Charles's Bridge at Stanford on Avon stands upstream of the modern road bridge.

from Daventry to Ashby St Legers and thence to Crick, avoiding the need to cross the tributary of the Nene altogether; a route that can be traced by road today.

A story is told of King Charles dining with Sir Thomas Cave of Stanford on Avon, crossing the bridge which is now known as King Charles's Bridge. At that time the Hall was south of the church on the opposite side of the road, east of the river which flows from north to south at this point, and it has been suggested that Charles rode south from his main line of march to come to dinner. If, however, he had come up through Yelvertoft, Sir Thomas's house would stand alongside his natural route to the Market Harborough road. Further, the total distance to be marched would be somewhat reduced. The bridge of the time can be seen alongside the modern road bridge. It is a slender affair, too narrow for wagons which would have had to ford the stream.

By Friday evening the Royalists were back in Leicestershire. Slingsby again:

'Wn we took our Quarters, we made ye head Quarters at Harborrow; our horse lay Quarter'd in Villages between us & ye enemy, who gave ym an Alarm, but presently were encounter'd wth a party of our horse, & chas'd untill they came to see where they had made their fire, in an open feild. Upon ye charge Liet. Coll. Sair, receiving a Shott near ye shouldier, was brought off to Harborrow, to Sr. Marmaduke Langdales Quarter.'

Sprigge recalls the incident in a different light.

'That evening we understood that the Van of the Enemies army was at

53

Harborough, the Rear within two miles of Naseby: and no sooner was the General got to his quarters, but tidings was brought him of the good service done by Colonel Ireton, in falling into the Enemies quarters, which they had newly taken up in Naseby Town; where he took many prisoners, some of the Princes Life-guard, and Langdales Brigade, and gave a sound alarm throughout the Enemies army (the confidence of the Enemy in possessing these quarters, grounded upon their slight esteem of this Army, and want of intelligence, was very remarkable.)'

For a more sober account we have Walker.

'Upon the 13 of June Intelligence being given of the Advance of Fairfax to Northampton, our Army retired back to Harborow with resolution to march the next Day to Melton Mowbray and so to Newark there to strengthen our Foot by Additions out of that and other adjacent Garrisons. But that Night an Allarum was given ...'

The two armies were now close to contact. Any hope the Royalists might have had of drawing off to the north had become unrealistic.

Far left: *Rapier and* **left:** *Broadsword both used by the cavalry.*

ROYAL ARMOURIES, LEEDS

Above: *Pollaxe, favoured by some cavalrymen because of its effectiveness against armour.*

ROYAL ARMOURIES, LEEDS

Chapter 3

THE APPROACH TO BATTLE, 14 JUNE 1645

Late in the night of the thirteenth to the fourteenth of June the Royalists were already on the move. News of the Parliamentarian strike on Friday evening on the patrol left at Naseby reached Charles in his lodgings at Lubenham some time around midnight and he made haste to convene a council of war in Market Harborough. He found Prince Rupert, it is said, in a house at the junction of Church Street and King's Road, later the King's Head Inn. There the King and his councellors considered what to do.

Sir Henry Slingsby is very brief in his recollection:

'This [the capture of the Royalists at Naseby] alarm'd ye King who lay at a place a little beyond Harborrow; thereupon command was given to draw forth; wch was ye 14th of June 1645, upon a Saturday; & by ye time it was light ye King himself was come unto ye Town, & all in readiness to march ...'

Sir Edward Walker was Secretary at War to the King and also Secretary to the Privy Council. He wrote a memoir for the information of Edward Hyde, later Earl of Clarendon, who wrote the principal history of the war from a Royalist viewpoint. Walker recalled:

'But that night an Allarum was given, that Fairfax with his Army was quartered within six Miles of us. This altered our design, and a Council being presently called, resolutions were taken to fight; and rather to march back and seek him out, than to be sought or pursued, contrary (as 'tis said) to Prince Rupert's Opinion; it being our unhappiness, that the Faction of the Court, whereof the most powerful were the Lord Digby and Mr John Ashburnham, and that of the Army ever opposed and were jealous of others.'

The Royalist Position

To the south of the River Welland and Market Harborough the hills rise steeply and the principal road to Northampton climbs to Great Oxendon before dropping into the valley to cross the little River Ise, which runs down from Clipston, and continuing through

Detail from the Ordnance Survey two-miles-to-the-inch map of 1908, showing the terrain over which the armies approached one another on the morning of 14 June. The road layout and land drainage are mostly 19th-century creations, but the hills show clearly, especially the ridge north of Naseby, running down to Kelmarsh and the main north/south road, and the ridge from East Farndon to Great Oxendon further north. Bodleian Library C17(36), Crown copyright

Kelmarsh. Fairfax's army, however, had been reported as being encamped overnight beyond Naseby and had scouts in that village, so an approach on a line further west, between Clipston and Sibbertoft, may have seemed possible, making a position on the western end of the hill, near the village of East Farndon, preferable. Moreover, in a countryside largely consisting of hedgeless, open fields, an enclosure then existed at Little Oxendon. The abandoned medieval village is on the northern side of the hilltop and the enclosures extended to the south-west, crossing what is now the East Farndon to Great Oxendon road in a strip about 600 yards (300m) wide centred on the modern Little Oxendon Farm and ending on the Great Oxendon to Clipston road at the modern Spinney Farm. Modern hedges follow the lines of that old enclosure.

The Royalists are reported to have left Market Harborough over Bloodymans Ford, where now a bridge alongside Welland Park carries the East Farndon road (B4036) south from its junction with the main road west from the town centre (A4304) towards Lubenham. The hill rises steeply along the narrow village street now and presumably it did then as well. Slingsby wrote:

'... we had not march'd a Mile out of Town, having taken a Hill whereupon a Chapell stood, but we could diserne ye enemy's horse upon another Hill about a Mile or two before us, wch was ye same on wch Naseby stood ...'

East Farndon church stands on the crown of the hill with the land

From the East Farndon to Great Oxendon road, the rear of the Royalist's original position, the communications mast next to the A14 close to New House Farm on the left and the spire of Naseby church, projecting over the trees on the horizon on the right, can be seen. Without trees to block the view, the Parliamentary vanguard on the Kelmarsh road north of Naseby would be visible.

Communications mast

Naseby spire

End of gully | Moot Hill | Sibbertoft Wood | Jugsholme
King's Standard | | | Bungalow

On the slope south of East Farndon and west of the Clipston road, the western flank is protected by the tree-filled gully running north to south (right to left) beyond which the white building of Jugsholme Bungalow can be seen. On the horizon to the left of the bungalow is the bulk of Sibbertoft Wood and the isolated tree to the left of that stands on the edge of King's Close on Moot Hill, where the King's Standard is said to have flown later in the day.

falling away abruptly to the west. The Clipston road curves around it, heading east to the junction with the Oxendon road at which point it turns south across gently sloping terrain. If the Royalists desired to occupy a front of about a mile (1.5km) centred on the Clipston Road, this was an acceptable position. The frontage is equal to that later occupied on Dust Hill before the battle began. The eastern flank could be anchored on the Little Oxendon close and infantry sent into the enclosures to guard the far flank. On the west a deep, steep-sided re-entrant cuts into the hill from the north past Jugsholme Farm giving bastion-like protection to the other flank. The disadvantage of the position is similar to that of the motte as a castle; there is no room at all for manoeuvre. You either stand here to receive attack or advance directly forward. Orderly retreat is out of the question as is any foray east or west from the flanks. It does not sound like the kind of position that would suit the aggressive Rupert, and perhaps this contributed to his willingness to abandon it. Another consideration which common sense suggests, although there is no documentary evidence that it was significant at the time, is the importance of the road coming north from Northampton through Kelmarsh. This was the route taken by the Royalists on their way to Daventry only a few days before and this was a likely route for the advancing Parliamentarians to follow. It passed on the other side, the east, of the Little Oxendon enclosures and thus could have been used in a encircling movement to outflank and get to the rear of the Royalist position, surrounding them entirely. An awareness of such vulnerability may have contributed to the decision to move. Walker thought well of the place, but reflected the uncertainty about the intentions of the enemy.

'In the Morning early being Saturday the 14 of June, all the Army was drawn up upon a rising ground of very great Advantage about a Mile from Harborow, which we left on our Back, and there put in order and dispose to give or receive the Charge... The Army thus disposed made a stand on that Ground, and about eight of the Clock in the Morning, it was a question whether the Intelligence were true ...'

Another church exists just off the main road north of Great Oxendon, overlooking the ridge and furrow of the ancient fields. Given the proximity of the Little Oxendon enclosures, the village of Great Oxendon and the steep hillsides, a case for this being Slingsby's 'Chappell' cannot be made. The question remains of how Rupert might have intended to deal with an advance up the main road by way of Kelmarsh, the route he had taken for Daventry, but the position described above appears to fit what evidence we have.

The Parliamentarian Position

Sir Thomas Fairfax was determined to bring the King to battle and had his army on the move from Guilsborough very early that Saturday morning. Joshua Sprigge reported:

'By five in the morning the Army was at a Rendezvouz near Naseby, where his Excellency [Fairfax] received Intelligence by our Spies, that the Enemy was at Harborough; with this further, that it was still doubtfull whther he meant to march away, or to stand us. But immediately the doubt was resolved: great Bodies of the Enemies horse were discerned on the top of the hill on this side of Harborough, which increasing more and more in our view, begat a confidence in the General, and the residue of the Officers that he meant not to draw away, as some imagined, but that he was putting his army in order, either there to receive us, or to come to us, to engage us upon the ground we stood: whilst the General was thus observing the countenance of the Enemy, directions were given to put the Army into such a posture, as that if the Enemy came on, we might take advantage of our ground, and be in readinesse to receive him; or if not, we might advance towards him.'

What Sprigge does not say is exactly where all this took place. However, if the possible routes from Guilsborough are considered, the options narrow. The Northampton to Leicester road through Spratton and Welford (A5199, which crosses the A14 at a junction) runs along a ridge between two streams. The direct route from Guilsborough to Naseby requires a descent from the hillside on the west, crossing the first stream, then up to the ridge and road, then down to the next stream before climbing the long ridge up to Naseby. Alternatively it is possible to follow the main road as far as Thornby, taking advantage of the superior carriageway, and then turn for Naseby with a lesser stream to cross. Thornby can also be reached by a road running due north from Guilsborough and turning to cross the two streams higher up their courses where they might be less troublesome. Or again, one could go on to the crossing with the Cold Ashby to Naseby road and then follow the low route over the water-meadows. This last might be acceptable for cavalry, but after so much rain the artillery and baggage train and almost certainly the foot would take one of the other two routes, bringing them to the south side of the village.

At this point no one knows what is going to happen next. The Royalists are at Harborough and possibly making off to Leicester or Newark and Fairfax is in pursuit. The horse naturally push forward towards Harborough on the road that leads to Kelmarsh and to Clipston which forks north-east of the village and of the windmill, immediately north of the bridge over the modern A14. From this point they can see across to the fields south of the Oxendon road, and there the King's army is deploying. The Parliamentary horse are at the edge of a steep hill that drops away towards Clipston and on a ridge that inclines gently towards Kelmarsh to the east and Mill Hill to the west. Behind them it rises slightly, dips down for a modest distance and rises once more to the position of the windmill, now occupied by the memorial obelisk. In the declivity a number of small groups of musket balls have been found, suggestive of accidental loss. It seems possible that it was here that Fairfax's officers set about the deployment of their troops as Sprigge describes.

The opposing sides had their first sight of each other early in the

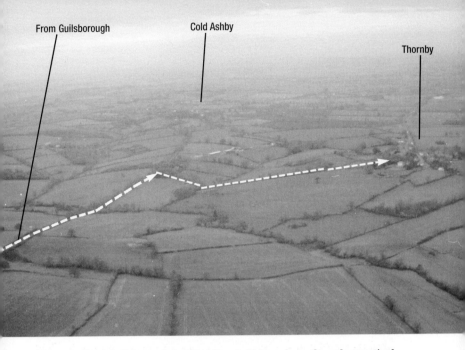

From Guilsborough   Cold Ashby   Thornby

The route from Guilsborough to Thornby would have been the only practical road for the Parliamentarian baggage train. The road on the left goes on a ridge to Cold Ashby, dipping into a little valley en route. On the right the modern A5199 comes along another ridge to Thornby and curves to the right to the A14 while a minor road heads for Cold Ashby and another crosses to the ridge on the left, this side of the farm buildings.

morning and as the day drew on their troops went on coming up from north and south. The roads south of Naseby and no doubt the flanking fields would have been full of marching pikemen and musketeers and the village with clattering horsemen. The artillery and baggage trains toiled up the muddy roadways, heading for the Kelmarsh road beyond Naseby in order to continue to Market Harborough. The area south, east and north of the village would bear this traffic, and when the baggage train halted it would almost certainly keep to this high, dry ground and avoid the water meadows and low fields to the west. To the south of the village, astride the Thornby road and as far as the Guilsborough road, is a fine, flat, high, dry area with excellent line of sight to the Kelmarsh turn near the modern New-house Farm on the right and to Mill Hill Farm on the left. This would have been a sensible place to halt the baggage train while the situation was assessed and to leave it when the army moved west to Mill Hill and thence forward in preparation for battle, but there is, as yet, no evidence to support this conjecture.

The Strengths of the Armies

The number of men taking the field has a close bearing on the credibility of the speculation about these initial positions and about the deployment of the forces for the battle itself. Clarendon's *History* draws on information supplied by Walker and on other sources to assert:

'The main body of the foot [of the Royalist army] was led by Lord Astley (whom the king had lately made a baron)

A view from above Thornby towards Naseby. On the left the curve of Breakey's Wood alongside the dark, ploughed field beyond, Lodge Farm can be seen. The Cold Ashby road runs along the far edge of that field to Naseby in the middle distance on the right. From the right of the picture the Thornby road climbs the ridge to Naseby and alongside it, showing as a pale area with trees on the roadside, is Mill Field, the location of the windmill that replaced the earlier one on the Obelisk site and a possible location for the baggage train.

consisting of about two thousand and five hundred foot. The right wing of horse, being about two thousand, was led by Prince Rupert; the left wing of horse, consisting of all the northern horse, with those from Newark (which did not amount to more than sixteen hundred), was commanded by Sir Marmaduke Langdale. In the reserve were the king's lifeguard, commanded by the Earl of Lindsey, and Prince Rupert's regiment of foot, both which did make very little above eight hundred; with the king's horse-guards, commanded by the Lord Bernard Stuart, which made that day about five hundred horse.'

This gives either 8,200 or 7,600 depending on the interpretation of the numbers of the lifeguards and Prince Rupert's foot which were either 800 taken together or 800 each. Other evidence suggests these are underestimates, possibly to put the subsequent defeat in a more kindly light. Glenn Foard, in 1995, calculated that the Royalists had

An emerging commander for the Parliamentarians, Oliver Cromwell, was to demonstrate his abilities as tactical general at the Battle of Naseby.

4,500 foot and 5,400 horse, giving a total of 9,900 men, while Stuart Reid, in 1998, suggests 5,000 foot and 5,450 horse for a total of 10,420 or so. It thus appears that something in the region of 10,000 will not be too wide of the mark. Lord John Belasyse, in the king's train, said: '... ours not exceeding 12,000 Horse and Foot'.

On the Parliamentary side records are more fragmented and vary in their reliability. Foard concludes that the total was 14,600 made up of 6,600 horse, 7,500 foot and 500 dragoons. Reid, on the other hand, suggests the much lower figure of 11,800. He points out that the numbers at Newport Pagnell can be fixed with some certainty at 7,031 foot and 3,014 horse, as reported in The Scottish Dove of 5 June. To this must be added the reinforcements of Vermuyden's horse and Cromwell's Ironsides, something between 2,500 and 3,000 men. Allowing some erosion of numbers of men in the march to Naseby at ten per cent or so, Reid arrives at 6,300 foot and 5,500 horse. In 1985 Peter Young, after extensive analysis of the constituent regiments, held that there were 14,000 Parliamentarians and 9,000 Royalists.

That the King's forces were outnumbered is beyond doubt. That they were so in a ratio of three to one as some writers have said is clearly wrong. It is tempting to opt for the lower number of Parliamentarians as it makes it easier to fit them into the available terrain, but that would be cheating! The concensus on the Royalists is clear at some 10,000 men and Fairfax may not have lost as many men as Reid suggests, so perhaps about 13,500 for Parliament is an acceptable hypothesis, in spite of Sprigge's observation:

'The battail was fought much upon equall advantage, whether you respect the numbers on each side, they being not 500 odds ...'

The Move to the West

Although each side had seen the other by, at the latest, eight o'clock in the morning, neither was sure what the other was planning to do. The Royalists had turned to face their foe in part because they worried that, as Clarendon says,

'... they might well apprehend the Scots' army in their face and Fairfax in their rear... and everybody believed that Fairfax's army was much dispirited by having failed in their two first enterprises ... and therefore that it was best to find them out whilst their fear was yet upon them.'

That was before they learned the discouraging news of the strength

Parliamentarians approaching their position of battle. ECWS

of the force Fairfax brought to Northampton, but now the enemy was so close the argument that they had best fight now regained its force. However, from the Oxendon road all they could see were horsemen on the ridge north-east of Naseby. Sprigge described the Parliamentarian puzzlement, and on the Royalist side Walker wrote:

'... one Francis Ruce the Scoutmaster was sent to discover;

A plot of the landscape profile on a direct line between the junction of the modern Naseby-Kelmarsh/Naseby-Clipston roads (Viewpoint B) and the East Farndon-Clipston/East Farndon-Great Oxenden roads (Viewpoint C); that is, the Parliamentarian and the Royalist viewpoints early on 14 June 1645. The dip, or dead ground, on the left is between the A14 and the Obleisk. The south-sloping Royalist position is clearly visible to their adversaries. There is also a good deal of dead ground, places out of enemy vision, between the positions.

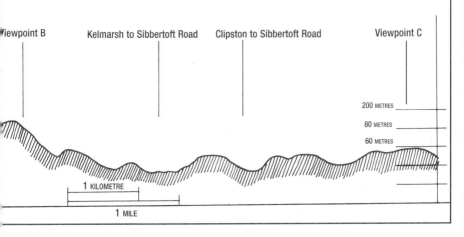

who in short time returned with a Lye in his Mouth, that he had been two or three miles forward, and could neither discover nor hear of the Rebels. This and a Report that they were retreated, made Prince Rupert impatient; and thereupon he drew out a Party of Horse and Musquetiers both to discover and engage them, leaving the Army in that Place and Posture.'

Accusations of incompetence at the least have been made against Ruce, and it is clear that he failed in his task, but a consideration of the nature of the landscape gives an understanding of the difficulties he faced. A profile of the country on the straight line between the junction of the Oxendon and Clipston roads at East Farndon in the north and the junction of the Clipston and Kelmarsh roads in the south is nothing like the symmetrical bowl the account of the hill-to-hill view suggests. Indeed, in Sprigge there is a remark that is hard to understand were symmetry the case:

'And whilest these things [the deployment of the troops] were in consultation and action, the Enemies Army, which before was the greatest part of it out of our view, by reason of the Hill that interposed, we saw plainly advancing in order towards us: and the winde blowing somewhat Westwardly, by the Enemies advance so much on their right hand, it was evident, that he designed to get the winde of us ...'

Exactly which hill interposed is hard to say, but the profile shows a number of candidates. It also shows that, the closer to Naseby you are in the valley, the less you can see of the ridge-top occupied by Fairfax's men. Today the A14 road passes across the ridge and can be seen quite clearly from the Oxendon road as high-sided trucks pass. From the valley floor they become invisible.

The reasons for the movement of both armies westwards to the hillsides above Broadmoor are not clear. A number of versions exist. Sprigge, for example, writing from the Parliamentary viewpoint, says that when it was thought the Royalists were trying to take the position to windward, which would result in gunsmoke obscuring Fairfax's men's view,

'... [the movement] occasioned the General to draw down into a large fallow field on the Northwest side of Naseby, flanked on the left hand with a hedge, which was a convenient place for us to fight the enemy in.'

Another story, recounted in *A Just Apology for an Abused Army* (1647) is that Cromwell encouraged Fairfax to move.

'Cromwell, who as though he had received direction from

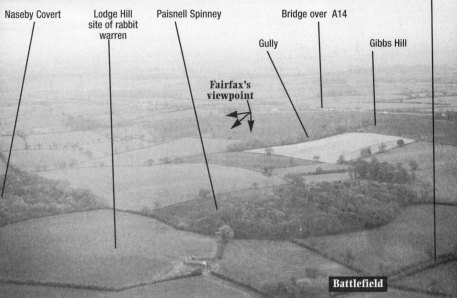

Naseby Covert

Lodge Hill
site of rabbit
warren

Paisnell Spinney

Bridge over A14

Gully

Gibbs Hill

**Fairfax's
viewpoint**

Battlefield

A view from above Broadmoor to the south east. The woods in the foreground are Naseby Covert, left, and Paisnell Spinney, right. Between them, with a farm building, is Lodge Hill, the site of the rabbit warren, and the road from Naseby to Sibbertoft runs right to left in the foreground. The far corner of the pale field, Tithwell, points towards the Clipston road bridge over the A14 along which trucks are going. The dark, ploughed field this side of the A14 is Gibbs Hill over which Fairfax had no trouble moving his army westwards. He would have viewed his enemies to the north from a point to the left of the pale-roofed building alongside the plough on the Clipston road. On the far side of Tithwell a line of trees from right to left marks a deep, steep gully, 'Happy Valley' as it is now known, the last remaining of several present at the time.

God himselfe, where to pitch the Battell; did advise, that the Batalia might stand upon such a ground, although it was being drawn up in another place, saying, "Let us I beseech you draw back to yonder hill, which will encourage the enemy to charge us, which they cannot doe in that place, without their absolute ruine".'

The problems of mounting an attack on Fairfax from below was also cited by Slingsby on the Royalist side:

'... after prayers being said, Prince Rupert draws forth a good body of horse, & advanceth towards ye enemy, where he sees their horse marching up on ye side of ye Hill to yt place where after they imbattl'd their whole army: but being hindred of any nearer approach, by reason ye place between us & ym, was full of burts [holes] & Water, we wheel'd about & by our guides

67

Detail from the Naseby Parish map of 1630. From the north east of the village the road, marked Kelmarsh Way and shown with dotted lines, passes the windmill (now the Obelisk) and curves through the legend Shepshoks Feild to run down the ridge to the east. The route of the modern Clipston road crosses the parish boundary in the centre of the curve above which the words `The Manner' are written left of a square labelled Scrawghill, which is the slope down which the road goes today. It is an unlikely route for wheeled traffic in 1645. The gully next to Tithwell shows below the field name. Suffolk Record Office HB56:2803, Neg.B1372

were brought upon a fair piece of ground, partly corn & partly heath, under Nasby ...'

Walker's account of Rupert's actions after the failed reconnaissance by Ruce says:

'But he [Rupert] had not marched above a Mile before he had certain Intelligence of their Advance, and saw their Van [vanguard]. Whereupon he drew nearer with his Horse, and sent back to have the Army march up to him; and either supposing by their motion, or being flattered into an Opinion they were upon a Retreat, he desired they should make haste. This made us quit our Ground of Advantage and in reasonable order to advance.'

So Walker and Slingsby both have it that Fairfax moved first, as does *A Just Apology*, while Sprigge thinks Rupert initiated the movement. The story of Cromwell's advice rings true, but regardless of the cause, the effect was to bring both armies westwards. The Royalists would have to come south far enough to clear the head of the Jugsholme Farm re-entrant, passing between the site of the modern Newbold Farm and Clipston village. They would have to avoid Nobold closes, the enclosed parcels of land astride the Clipston to Sibbertoft road on the east side of the ridge, against the parish boundary. Here, before the road gains the plateau which begins in effect at Lowe Farm, a deserted village lay south of the road and an enclosed field north of it. The Clipston parish field names are Nobold and Nobold Meadow on the south and Englands, a common corruption of Inlands, to the north. From Lowe Farm to the village of Sibbertoft and south to Dust Hill the land is virtually flat, allowing swift movement over the open fields and along the road to the south boundary of the parish, the same road as runs there today. Sibbertoft was already partially enclosed at this time, a process to be completed in 1650, and it may be that some hedges close to the village obstructed movement or could be used for cover.

The King's men had a fair way to come, up to two and a half miles (4km), but they no doubt formed their line of march from their battalia or battle formations as laid down in the contemporary drill books and would have little difficulty reforming on Dust Hill. Their artillery and baggage, on the other hand, was constrained to keep to the road down to Clipston and then up through the narrows at Nobold to Sibbertoft where the baggage train halted in the fields between Lowe Farm and the footpath that comes north from the junction of the Naseby and Kelmarsh roads.

The field to the north of Lowe Farm that now has an Ordnance Survey triangulation pillar in it is known as King's Close and the hill on which it lies as Moot Hill. Tradition says the king's standard was raised here. Given the challenge of moving the army into the low valleys and back up to the Sibbertoft plateau, raising a flag here to mark the line of march and show a rallying point makes sense, even if it cannot be proved.

That the time was available for the Royalists to make this move, so much further than their adversaries had to go, can be explained in part by the fact that Fairfax's forces were not fully drawn up and in part because the Parliamentarians were keen to provoke an attack. They almost certainly moved west along the broad ridge now occupied in part by the new A14, over Gibbs Hill to Mill Hill. The land is significantly more hilly north of this line. From Mill Hill, going north, they would have to descend into a little valley before making the short climb to the ridge overlooking Broadmoor and starting preparations for battle.

In June 1645 the whole area would have been teeming some 23,500 fighting men of both sides plus countless numbers of camp followers. Here some pikemen and musketeers belonging to Prince Rupert's Blew Regiment of Foote (re-enactors) muster for drill.

Chapter 4

THE BATTLE, 14 JUNE 1645 – THE FORMAL PHASE

The high land of Naseby and Sibbertoft parishes is mostly covered in Boulder Clay topped with red Northamptonshire Sand, except where streams have cut down into the underlying clays. In the north the Hothorpe Hills overlook the Welland valley. At the time of the battle some fields close to Sibbertoft village had been enclosed, but most of the land was still under open field cultivation. Indeed, it remained so in Naseby until the nineteenth century. Writing in 1792, the Reverend John Mastin described his parish.

'... not a hedge, or a tree for more than a mile together, a few scattered thorns only and patches of gorse or furze...

'This extensive, and almost boundless open field, consists of about two thirds pasture, and one of arable, the whole very improveable by inclosure. The farmers, twenty-one in number who keep teams, support constantly four working blacksmiths, two working wheelwrights, besides carpenters; one collar-maker, and of course many labourers; six shoemakers, two butchers, and one baker.

'The mode of husbandry is regular, as to the culture; the lordship being divided into three parts, not by fences, but by marks made in the ground, called field-marks, so that there may be said to be three fields; viz. one, wheat, rye, and barley; one beans and oats; and one fallow... The stock in the field consists of two thousand eight hundred sheep, three hundred and sixty of the cow kind, and about three hundred mares ...'

A report by Mr W. Pitt on the state of agriculture in Northamptonshire of 1809 described the landscape thus:

'The lower parts a moist rough pasture, with furze, rushes and fern abounding; the rest of the field a strong brown deep loam, in the usual wheat and bean culture... The avenues across the field are zig-zag, as chance has directed, with the hollows and sloughs unfilled, except with mire.'

In addition to these reports some one and a half centuries after the battle, there survives a map of Naseby parish dating from 1630 (see page 72). It has been photocopied and photographed at various times in the twentieth century and only skilled forensic examination will

71

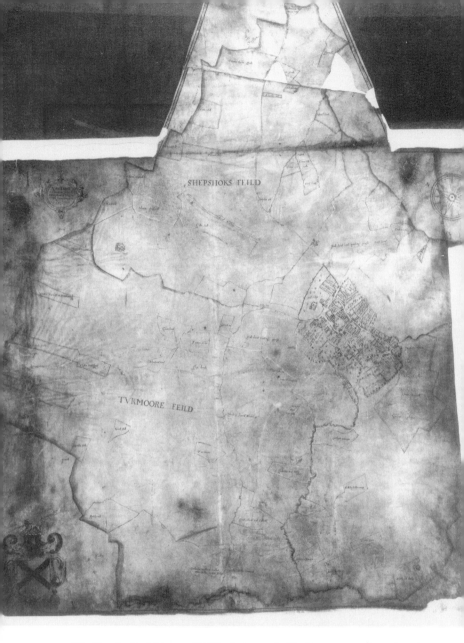

The Naseby Parish map of 1630, photographed before over-zealous cleaning reportedly obscured some features of interest. The boundaries on the north and east match those of modern maps. The areas squared off and labelled were not actually enclosed with hedges, but are simply identified here for administrative purposes; the country was almost entirely open, with hedges and ditches to prevent livestock straying into neighbouring parishes.

determine exactly what it showed originally. The authors have examined copies made since the Second World War and a photograph of the original map, assuming there is only one original, in the Suffolk archives is reproduced here. On this map the roads are sketched in, the main purpose of the document being to specify land and property rights. As already mentioned the road to Kelmarsh is shown clearly with a dotted edging, running past the windmill and through Shepshoks Field before turning to follow the ridge to the east. Equally robust in representation is the road from the north-eastern corner of the village going due east and marked Haselbech Way. Another road, abandoned by 1820 but still to be detected as a hollow-way, entered the village on the east and shows only as two words, Thornby Way, on the Suffolk map.

At the south-eastern corner the roads from Guilsborough and Thornby are not shown at all, but they are on the Northampton Records Office copy. To the south-west the road for Cold Ashby cannot be seen on the Suffolk copy but is shown on the Northampton copy passing close by a block of land labelled Ashby Way. On the west the strong, curving line of Carvell's Lane, well to the north of the main stream of the River Avon, shows as a pale trace on the Suffolk map and as a strong line on other copies. A lesser stream can also be seen originating from the road immediately south of Hall Close at the north of the village and running to the zig-zag boundary just above the lane and following it down to the river. There is no road to Welford other than Carvell's Lane and the road to Sibbertoft shows only as a tentative, pale line just west of the division between Shepshoks Field and Turmoore Field. This was, perhaps, one of Mr Pitt's 'avenues'. The boundaries here are those of the parish at the time and are exactly the same as they are today, so modern maps can be related directly to this. In the north, close to the Sibbertoft boundary and looking like an eye on a sketchy face forming the edge of Shepshoks Field, is Warren House. Mastin wrote:

'Upon a dry hill north of the village, called lodge hill, was formerly a rabbit warren, upon which was a house, as may be seen by the spot on which it stood; the house itself is entirely demolished.'

To the north-east of the warren the distinctive wedge of the north-eastern boundary of the nineteenth-century plantation of Naseby Covert permits a precise fix on a modern map. Finds of nails on the hilltop confirm the location of Warren House as being the field still known as Lodge Hill.

Site of modern Cromwell Memorial

Road built in 1820

The Naseby Enclosure map of 1820. The parish boundary assists comparison with the 1630 map. Top right, is the sharp point of modern Naseby Covert from which a boundary approximating to the division between the old, great fields runs south. Due south of the village and the Churchwardens' land a tiny drawing of a windmill marks modern Mill Field.

M WESTAWAY COLLECTION

The parish was mapped again when the fields were enclosed by Act of Parliament in 1820. Many features can be recognised, as well as changes and additions. The Clipston Road leaves the Kelmarsh road in what is labelled as Oldmill Field, clearly what was Shepshocks Field, and the three roads from the south of the village run as they do today. Enclosure has made a straight line of Carvell's Lane and moved it further from the line of the river at the time, while, from the north-eastern corner, a road now runs to Welford and an entirely new road strikes due north to join the older road in Sibbertoft parish. The change from the surveyor's ruled line of road to the gentle meander of the old road is immediately evident to the modern motorist. Missing from all these is the line of the modern A14 which almosts touches Carvell's Lane's ruler-straight, 1820 line in the west, crosses the Welford road one third of the way from the western edge of the long rectangle of Fitzgerald holding alongside the Sibbertoft road, and cuts just south of the junction of the Clipston and Kelmarsh roads before crossing the latter. The researches carried out by Fitzgerald, the subject of his correspondence with Thomas Carlyle, were made on this rectangle of land. While, regrettably, the modern road crosses the battle area it does not actually infringe on the terrain on which the main fighting took place, all of which is north of the new, four-lane highway.

The Parliamentary Battle Lines

There are a number of sources of information from which a reasonable description of the initial positions of both armies can be derived. Sprigge's *Anglia Rediviva* of 1647, his history of the New Model Army, was illustrated with Streeter's depiction of the armies 'as they were drawn into severall bodyes, at the Battayle at Nasbye'. On the Royalist side Sir Bernard de Gomme produced a series of diagrams of the major battles of the war. These taken together give a great deal of information, although the former is an artistic interpretation and the latter a technical diagram; each having its limitations. Written accounts of the regiments present and calculations of frontages derived from them and from the pictures have been published by a number of authorities and, finally, the work of plotting the presence of shot found by metal detection has been undertaken by two of the authors of this book as well as by one or two others. This evidence has then been subjected to scrutiny in the ground itself.

Sprigge gives a detailed account of the action taken after the decision to draw down to the fallow field from their first position on the Kelmarsh road.

> 'And indeed seeing [the enemy's] resolution to advance upon us, we took the best advantage we could of the ground, possessing the ledge of a Hill, running from East to West; upon which our Army being drawn up, fronted towards the Enemy.

North of the hill on which Mill Hill Farm stands, separated from it by a modest valley, is the ridge which fits Sprigge's description. In a letter to Carlyle, Fitzgerald drew a diagram and labelled the ridge, from left to right, Red Hill, Cloisterwell and Lodge Hill. The latter is the location of the warren and several fields today carry the word 'Cloister' or a variant of it in their names. Thus, while the hill does not actually have a name, we will refer to it as Cloister in this text. Sprigge's ledge can be seen to the south of the monument that stands west of the Naseby to Sibbertoft road on the northern face of the hill. Today a hedge runs along it, but the abrupt incline is clear and the advantage of occupying the ground, Cloister, above and south of it evident. Sprigge goes on:

> 'But considering it might be of advantage to us to draw up our Army out of sight of the Enemy; who marched upon a plain ground towards us: we retreated about an hundred paces from the ledge of the Hill, that so the Enemy might not perceive in what form our battell was drawn, nor see any confusion therein, and yet we to see the form of their battell; to which we could conform ourselves for advantages, and recover the advantage of the Hill when we pleased, which accordingly we did. The enemy perceiving this retreat thought (as since they had confessed) we were drawing off to avoid fighting ...'

Field names in the north of Naseby Parish and south of Broadmoor. These fields post-date the battle which was fought when this was open country, but, although some hedges have gone, they are mostly there today and help in specifying locations on the ground for the convenience of visitors and students.

M WESTAWAY COLLECTION CROWN COPYRIGHT

In 1855 Naseby was still a village of cob, mud and straw, houses. Only two survive today, in the High Street, and there is another in Guilsborough. In 1791 the church tower was adorned with a globe, more recently replaced with a spire. M WESTAWAY COLLECTION

A number of points arise from this account. The withdrawal appears to have been in part to conceal the confusion resulting from the inexperience of about half of the men of the New Model Army and perhaps also to spare them the tense experience of watching the Royalists march south across the Sibbertoft plain to Dust Hill. It may be that Royalist commentators on Rupert's generalship confused this manouevre with the reported semblance of retreat from the Kelmarsh road earlier in the day, for the sequence of the narratives from different hands varies confusingly. A retreat of 100 paces would have taken Fairfax's front line back beyond the line of the south hedge of the field immediately behind the monument, East Cloister Hill, and beside the Sibbertoft road. The formations would be, if six deep, about eighteen feet from front to rear and if eight deep twenty-four feet, so allowing for the gap needed, the next regiment in support would be on the south-facing slope of the hill, in the little valley north of Mill Hill in which Barn Close is situated. From the fall of shot detected it seems likely that the front line was approximately along the hedge on the southern side of East Cloister Hill as it is north of this hedge and about half way across the field that the eastern end of the band of shot- fall was found. This is consistent with the Parliament line moving forward a little as battle was joined. In considering this it is necessary to keep in mind that, at the time, none of the trees or hedges were present on the fronts of the two armies.

Sprigge gives this account of the Parliamentarian battle order.

'The General [Fairfax], together with the Major-General [Skippon], put the several Brigades of Foot into order: having committed the Ordering of the Horse to Lieutenant-General Cromwell, who did obtain from the General, That seeing the Horse were neere 6000 and were to be fought in two wings; His Excellency would please to make Col. Ireton Commissary gen. of horse [i.e. second in command of horse] and appoint him to command the Left Wing, that day, the command of the Right wing being as much as the Lieutenant-General could apply himself to. Which being granted by the General the Lieutenant-General assigned him five Regiments of horse, a Division of 200 Horse of the Association, for that wing; and the Dragoons to line the forementioned hedge, to prevent the enemy from annoying the Left flank of the Army. In the mean time the Lieutenant-General having six Regiments of Horse with him for the Right wing, disposed them according as the place gave leave. And the form of the whole <u>Battail you have here inserted</u>.

See spread on pages 80 and 81

79

Streeter's depiction of the opposing armies at Naseby 'here inserted' as in Sprigge's account (previous page). The topography is not to be relied upon.
M WESTAWAY COLLECTION

AND FOOT OF HIS MAJESTIES, AND
severall bodyes, at the Battayle at NASBYE;
day of June 1645

Sulby Parish   Tree tops indicate valley   Cloister   Prince Rupert's Farm

Royalist troops

Parliamentary troops

From Mill Hill field, Cromwell's possible viewpoint on the westward extension of Gibbs Hill. The treetops just beyond the hedge in the foreground show the valley north of Mill Hill and south of Cloister. Cloister is the other side of the road in the middle distance with Prince Rupert's Farm beyond. The pale fields far off on the left are in Sulby parish.

From Streeter the front line can be seen to be, from the right, the Life Guard, half of Sir Robert Pye's and Col Whalleys regiments, half of Col Rossiter's squeezed in immediately to their right rear, in the second line half of Col Fiennes's, the rest of Pye's and Col Sheffields division and to their rear in reserve the rest of Rossiter's and of Fiennes's and the Association horse, a Suffolk formation under Col Gourdon. In all a rather makeshift arrangement occasioned by the difficulty of the ground.

The fact that the whole army had moved to the left meant that Cromwell had to fit his men into what remained of the viable front, for the foot were occupying the coherent hilltop in the centre and this right flank was constrained by a stream running down the face of the hills north of the Kelmarsh road and with Gibbs Hill, as it is marked on the parish map, to its west. Today the stream passes along the east side of Naseby Covert forming a side of the wedge shape mentioned in the last chapter. The area is further split by the stream issuing from the valley north of Mill Hill, turning north to form part of the boundary of Turmoore and Shepshoks fields and then flowing south of Lodge Hill, on which the rabbit warren was, to form the other side of the wedge shaped half of Naseby Covert on the parish boundary. The eastern side of the field boundary is now occupied by Paisnell Spinney which, like Naseby Covert, was not there at the time. Accounts of the movement of the cavalry suggest that Whalley's horse was not troubled by the rabbit warren but that the other three squadrons were.

From the top of Gibbs Hill the view to Dust Hill and beyond to Sulby Hedges is uninterrupted once the spinney, trees and hedges have been erased by imagination. From here, from the top of the forward edge of Mill Hill, the dead ground in which the parish boundary lies is not evident. Cromwell may well have elected to stay this far south, overseeing his front line of horse on a level with Fairfax's foot and with the whole of the Parliamentary army in view. Away on Dust Hill, before they advanced down onto Broadmoor, he would be able to see the complete Royalist force as well.

In the centre of the line were the infantry with Fairfax's regiment on the right in the front line, then Col Monatague's, Pickering's, Sir Hardres Waller's and finally Skippon's. To their rear were the reserves of Rainsborough, Hammond and part of Pride's and as a rearguard the rest of Pride's men. Forward of them all was a Forlorn Hope of musketeers to break up the enemy advance and, if they survived, supposed to race back for shelter amongst the main body. The musket shot discovered lay in a belt about 2,000 feet wide, whereas Foard's calculation of frontage (if files were six deep) is 2,850 feet. What the fuss was actually about in the deployment of the troops here, and exactly why they fell back to do so is only explained by Sprigge in terms of keeping it secret, but what the deployment involved was is not mentioned. Given the fact that the broad, flat ridge, on which a line of field-names share the word Cloister, is approximately 2,000 feet wide, perhaps it was necessary to re-conform the infantry in eight-deep files, as is the standard advocated by Barriffe in his manual, in order to fit them in. In any case, the best conjecture we can offer is that the front line ran from a point on the modern Sibbertoft road due west, north of the site of the wind pump on Cloister, for about 2,000 feet. From the monument, even if the hedges were removed, the foot could not have been seen by the Royalists except as the tops of pikes on the horizon. From down on Broadmoor, at the foot of the slope on which the monument stands, they could not be seen at all. Writing from the Royalist point of view Slingsby remarked:

Dust Hill   Long Hold Spinney   Broadmoor   Re-entrant

Royalist troops

Parliamentary troops

From the northern hedge of West Cloister Hill, looking over Broadmoor to the north east and, on the skyline, Long Hold Spinney. The land slopes away to the east, the right, to form a shallow indentation in the west/east ledge of Cloister.

'... they lay without our sight, having ye Hill to cover ym, & appear'd no more to us yn wt they had drawn out in Battalio upon ye side of Naseby Hill ...'

So it seems that the Royalists had no very clear idea of their enemy's numbers.

One other aspect of the Parliamentary infantry position emerges from viewing the ground in an area which, at the time of writing, is not accessible to the public, being private land. About three-fifths of the way from the road to the western end of the line of the Parliamentary foot a re-entrant, a shallow bite of a valley, cuts south into West and Middle Cloister fields. It is not particularly impressive, but at the point at which it meets the hedge continuing from the side of the footpath to the Cromwell Monument, it extends roughly eighty feet (25m) back into the hillside and is about the same in width. It is some six to eight feet (2m) lower than the flanking ground. From the north, at a distance, this is visible as the dip in the east-west hedge-line centred on the boundary between the fields called West and Middle Cloister Hill. This suggests that Waller's regiment faced the re-entrant, perhaps extending a little to the east of it, and Skippon's was to the left or west of it, the former facing a gentler slope and the latter potentially isolated on a modest peninsula, now the field called Clouster Well. Attacking troops would have been inclined to get

84

bunched in the funnel of the re-entrant and their front would become wedge-shaped. The discontinuity in the terrain may also have encouraged Skippon to put the Forlorn Hope forward of the re-entrant as shown in Streeter's picture.

The left wing of horse consisted of Ireton's, Vermuyden's (commanded by Major Huntingdon) and Butler's with, in the second line, the rest of the Association (Suffolk) horse, Fleetwood's and Rich's regiments. They were able to adopt a conventional deployment, having more room in part because they arrived first. Their frontage would be limited by the right-angle of the parish boundary with Sulby, for the hedge that now runs behind the monument reaches the parish boundary at the point at which the Sulby Hedges come from the north to turn westwards, the corner of East Sulby Hill. If they were planning to charge their enemy, Ireton's men would not want to deploy further west than the flank created by those hedges.

The dragoons were also allocated to the left and, presumably after briefing Ireton in his new command, Cromwell gave Col Okey personal instructions for the deployment of these troops. Okey wrote:

'I was half a mile behinde in a Meadow giving my men Ammunition, and had not the Lieutenant Gen. come presently & caused me with all speed to mount my men & flank our left Wing, which was the King's right Wing of horse; where was

Parliamentarian commander Okey advanced west of the Sulby Parish hedges. Shot detection suggests that Prince Rupert's musketeers drove Okey's men back from the dotted area to the solid black area. It was from here that Okey's dragoons fired on Rupert's charging cavalry.

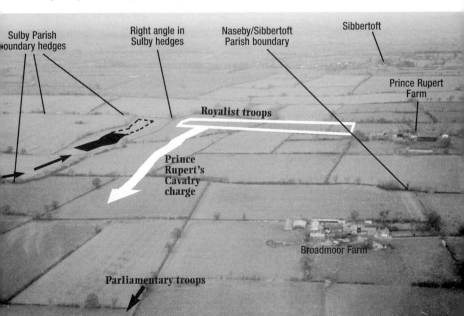

Sulby Parish boundary hedges

Right angle in Sulby hedges

Naseby/Sibbertoft Parish boundary

Sibbertoft

Prince Rupert Farm

Royalist troops

Prince Rupert's Cavalry charge

Broadmoor Farm

Parliamentary troops

Prince Maurice, who charged at the head of his Regiment ...'
It thus seems probable that Okey was in the little valley between Mill Hill and Cloister when Cromwell came upon him. Okey's dragoons then moved to take position behind the hedges mention by Sprigge. The fields of Sulby were probably enclosed when the village was abandoned sometime between 1377 and 1428 and hedges separated them from the Naseby and Sibbertoft lands. Okey's position was long assumed to be a forward projection of the main Parliamentarian line, but the written records become much easier to interpret in the light of the archaeological evidence. From shot finds it is clear that Okey actually means that he went to flank the Royalist horse and so was much further north than previously thought, actually threatening Rupert's men on their own ground. Their location is discussed below as part of the action.

The space occupied by these men has been painstakingly calculated by a number of scholars, most recently by Glenn Foard (*Naseby: The Decisive Campaign*, 1995, pages 238-242). The information is valuable but not definitive. As mentioned above, it may be at variance with physical evidence. No matter what the theory may be, the terrain and the finds of shot are facts which have to be the foundation of a reconstruction of events.

The Royalist Positions

The King's men had to move a good deal further than their adversaries; some two and a half miles as opposed to one mile for the foot soldiers. Prince Rupert with some horse and musketeers had gone forward from the Farndon position, but it is not clear how far before they decided to make the move westwards to the Sibbertoft plateau. The land is almost flat from Sibbertoft village to the edge of Dust Hill with a gentle westward tilt, and it narrowed from the west where the enclosure of Sulby had its northern boundary. From the road coming south from Sibbertoft village, after just a few yards, at the point it turns easterly for Kelmarsh, it is possible to see Cloister even with modern hedges in place and, by the time Rupert had gained this plateau at any point between Sibbertoft and Dust Hill, he would have seen the Parliamentary cavalry arriving on Cloister. Slingsby, the Royalist diarist and witness of these events, wrote:

'The prince having taken his ground began to put in order horse in sight of ye enemy, who were now come to ye top of ye Hill, & begin to draw down their Regiments upon ye side of ye hill: where they took their ground to imbattle their forces:

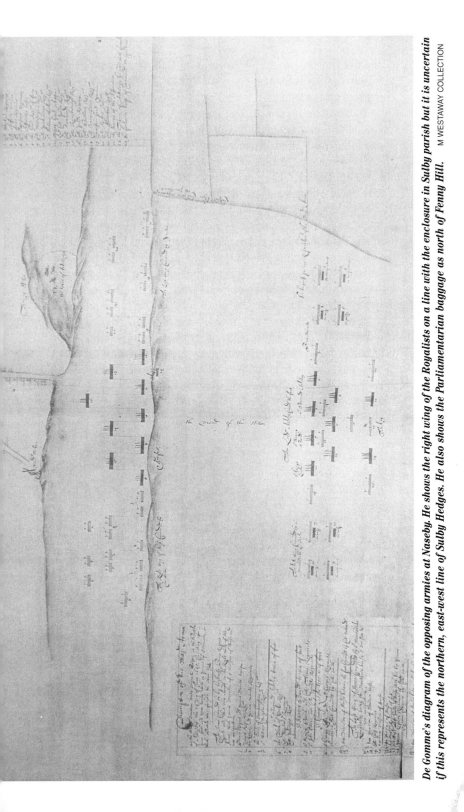

De Gomme's diagram of the opposing armies at Naseby. He shows the right wing of the Royalists on a line with the enclosure in Sulby parish but it is uncertain if this represents the northern, east-west line of Sulby Hedges. He also shows the Parliamentarian baggage as north of Fenny Hill. M WESTAWAY COLLECTION

immediately he sends to ye King, to hasten away ye foot, & Cannon, wch were not yet come off ye Hill where they first made ye randevous ...'

The Royalists came up as discussed in the previous chapter to reform on a line probably at something of an angle to their opponents. Here there is no shot-fall to assist in establishing the line in full as what there is relates to fighting later on as the Royalists fell back, except for that on the west. The ridge on which the modern Prince Rupert's Farm stands slopes into a shallow valley down which the Sulby Hedges run southwards from the corner of their east/west northern edge. This is also the parish boundary and is thus easy to see on a modern map. Inside the north end of the enclosure the ground is flat for a distance before sloping away south-east. On this area a significant concentration of musket shot has been found, suggesting that Okey's men initially came this far forward to the very flank of Rupert's horse. Okey said:

'But by that time [at which] I could get my men to light [dismount], and deliver up their Horses, in a little close, the Enemy drew towards us: which my men perceiving, they with shooting and rejoycing received them, although they were encompassed on the one side with the King's Horse, and on the other side with Foot and Horse to get the Close; but it pleased God that we beat off both the Horse and Foot on the left, and the right Wing, and cleared the field, and kept our ground...'

Okey's reports are not models of clarity, but examination of evidence on the ground suggests that his dragoons were seen as they rushed up the hill behind the hedge and that action was taken to oppose them. A rain of musketry through the hedge drove them back down the hill, for the finds are compatible with incoming fire on them from their left, that is, from the north where the musketeers with the cavalry of the Royalist right wing were, according to de Gomme, positioned. The encompassment spoken of is thus seen to be by musketeers and pistol-firing horse outside the hedge on their north. It also places Rupert's right wing adjacent to the north-eastern corner of Sulby Hedges. There has also been found a great arc of shot curving from the north-eastern corner of Sulby Hedges and reaching some 300 yards (275m) into Broadmoor, in line with the eastern side of Fourteen Acres, at the parish boundary. A more positive sign of outgoing fire from a force ensconced behind the hedges would be hard to describe. The picture of the dragoons being repulsed by fire from the north, pushed down the slope, lining the hedge and firing

Dust Hill Farm   Prince Rupert's Farm   Cloister   East Sulby Hill

Parliamentary troops

Royalist troops

Rupert's viewpoint from the north-eastern corner of Sulby Hedges, looking south east. On the skyline left, Long Hold Spinney with Dust Hill Farm and a little to the right, Prince Rupert's Farm; the Royalist line. On the right of the picture, beyond the pond, is the pale roof of a building on Broadmoor Farm and the open land of East Sulby Hill, Ireton's position, is on the horizon.

back at their attackers on the north and east into the flank of the advancing Royalist cavalry is clear.

From the corner of Sulby Hedges the spine of the ridge runs just south of due east, past Prince Rupert's Farm, through Dust Hill Farm and into the southern end of Long Hold Spinney which was not, of course, planted at that time. According to de Gomme's diagram the deployment was, from the Royalist right, as follows: five divisions of horse and 200 musketeers with Prince Rupert's, Prince Maurice's and the Queen's in the front line and the Earl of Northampton's and Sir William Vaughan's in the second. The foot, under Lord Astley, consisted of Sir Bernard Astley's tertia, made up of the Duke of York's and Col Hopton's in the front line and Col Paget's in the second, Sir Henry Bard's tertia of his own and Col Thomas's in the front line and Sir John Owen's and Col Gerrat's in the second; and Sir George Lisle's tertia with his own and St George's regiments in the front line and Col Smith's Shrewsbury foot in the second. The left wing of horse under Sir Marmaduke Langdale has three divisions of the Northern Horse in the front line and another in the second with Col Cary's. Col Howard's three divisions of horse were placed amongst the infantry and, to the rear in reserve with the King, were

89

two divisions of the Newark horse on the wings, the King's and Prince Rupert's regiments of foot right and left of the King's Life Guard of Horse in the centre.

The Battle on the Western Flank

Possibly as a result of Okey's sudden appearance in the Sulby close, the Royalist right was first to move, at about ten o'clock. As Slingsby reported:

'... they had possess'd an Hedge upon our right wing wch they had lin'd with Musqueteers to Gall our horse, (as indeed they did) before we could come up to charge theirs.'

Being thus galled, it seems only sensible for the front line of Rupert's horse to move forward, leaving the musketeers to deal with Okey. This only had the effect of pushing him down hill so that, Slingsby again,

'It fell upon Prince Ruport to charge at yt disadvantage, &

This re-enactment gives some idea of what a battle of that time would have looked like as Englishmen fought against each other in general affray. ECWS many of ye Regiment wound'd by shot from ye hedge before we could joyne with theirs on yt wing ...'

As noted above, the detected shot makes the fight on the western flank very clear. From the Parliamentarian side the forward movement was harder to understand. Sprigge wrote:

'Upon the approach of the Enemies Right wing of Horse, our left wing drawing down the brow of the hill to meet them, the Enemy comming on fast, suddenly made a stand, as if they had not expected us in so ready a posture: Ours seeing them stand, made a little stand also, partly by reason of some disadvantage of the ground, and untill the rest of the Divisions of Horse might recover their stations.'

The reasons for pausing could have been to regroup after being thrown into some disarray by broken and boggy ground but on the Royalists side it might also have been to allow the rest of the cavalry and the foot to catch up after the enemy dragoons had forced a premature start, not to mention the hazard of the hedge and ditch intended to prevent cattle straying over the parish boundary.

If the opposing sides were schooled in the tactics reported by J.B. in 1661, no shot-fall is to be expected to help us locate the cavalry fight, as they would have attacked 'with the Swords point' and saved their pistols for later use. Sprigge reported the result.

'... the Enemy advanced again, whereupon our Left wing sounded a Charge, and fell upon them: The three right hand divisions of our left wing [Ireton's and likely a part of Vermuyden's] made the first onset, and those divisions of the Enemy opposite them, received the charge: the two left hand Divisions [Butler's] of the Left wing did not advance equally, but being more backward, the opposite Divisions of the Enemy

91

A cavalry action. ECWS

advanced upon them.

The Parliamentary left enjoyed some success, for as Sprigge goes on to say,

'Of the three right hand Divisions (before mentioned) which advanced, the middlemost [one of Vermuyden's] charged not home, the other two coming to a close Charge, routed the two opposite Divisions of the Enemy... That Division of the enemies which was between, which the other Division of ours should have charged, was carried away in the disorder ... one of those Divisions of our Left wing that did rout the front of the enemy, charged the Reserve too, and broke them ...'

But it was not to last. Northampton's Regiment was coming on, despite what Okey could do. He said:

'When as the King's Horse had driven our men a mile before them on the left Wing at their first coming on; then wee discovered many of the King's Regiment, by reason that they came somewhat neare unto us; before ever they discharged a Pistoll at any Horse; and had not wee by God's providence been there, there had been but few of Colonel Butler's Regiment left. After this wee gave ourselves up for lost men, but wee resolved every man to stand to the last.'

Even so, the result was as described by Sprigge:

'... the other Reserves of the enemy came on, and broke those Divisions of ours that charged them; the Divisions of the left hand of the right [left?] wing were likewise overborn, having much disadvantage, by reason of pits of water, and other pieces of ditches that they expected not, which hindered them in the order to Charge. The Enemy having worsted our left wing, pursued their advantage ...'

Edward Wogan of Okey's Dragoons added to this:

'... the King's horse ... routed us clear beyond our carriages ... a great many of our horse went clear away to Northampton and could never be stopt.'

Rupert had broken through, but had not destroyed, Ireton's force on the left. George Bishop, a Parliamentarian, wrote from Great Glen two days later:

'... our left wing of Horse, and of Foot, and their right, first to engage; where was most terrible dispute, at length the fury of the Enemy caused two Regiments of Horse to give ground a little, the rest stood, the retreat was upon Major Generall Skippon's Regiment, being the utmost of that wing ...'

Ireton's own division was still there, as is related below, and sufficient of his reserves held on to take up position on the right wing in due course, so while they had been 'worsted' for the time being, they were still to be reckoned with.

The Centre – the Foot

The Royalist infantry had already moved forward with some zest. The Parliamentary force came forward onto the top of Cloister at the same time. Sprigge's narrative goes:

'Upon the Enemies approach, the Parliament's army marcht up to the brow of the hill [from the reverse slope?], having placed a Forlorn of Foot (musqueteers) consisting of about 300 down the steep of the hill towards the enemy, somewhere more than Carbine shot from the Main battail, who were ordered to retreat to the battail, whensoever they should be hard pressed by the enemy. The Enemy this while marched up in good order,

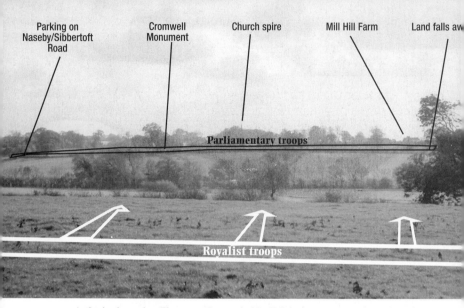

Parking on Naseby/Sibbertoft Road · Cromwell Monument · Church spire · Mill Hill Farm · Land falls aw[ay]

Parliamentary troops

Royalist troops

Astley's viewpoint: The ground occupied by Fairfax's army, seen from the private road to Prince Rupert's Farm. On the extreme left the Naseby to Sibbertoft road at the parking place for the Cromwell Monument. In the centre, on the skyline above the trees, Naseby Church spire. From the parking place a hedge runs across the darker fields and just right of a tree growing out of it is the Monument, a pillar with a ball on top. To the right, below Mill Hill Farm on the horizon, the land starts to fall towards the re-entrant.

with a great deal of gallantry and resolution, according to the form here inserted [Streeter's engraving].'

Sir Edward Walker saw the events from the Royalist side.

'Presently our Forces advanced up the Hill, the Rebels only discharging five Pieces [of artillery] at them, but over shot them, and so did their Musketeers. The Foot on either side hardly saw each other until they were within Carabine Shot, and so only made one Volley; ours falling in with Sword and butt end of Musquet did notable Execution; so much so I saw their Colours fall, and their Foot in great disorder.'

Quite how Walker was able to be sure that the musket shot and cannon balls all missed is unclear. What is known, for they have been found, is that a great number of musket shot subsequently lay in the soil on the forward slope of Cloister Hill, near the southern hedge line of the field south of the Cromwell Monument, presumably the result of the discharge before the two sides met hand-to-hand. The Royalist success was on their right, the Parliamentary left, where Skippon's regiment was pushed back and where Skippon himself was wounded, according to one report, by one of his own musketeers who

94

was wheeling into position. Edward Wogan, who served with Okey, wrote:

'The King's foot got ground apace, upon our foot being discouraged by our horse running away, and by Major-General Skippon's being desperately wounded; insomuch that all our foot gave ground and were in a manner running away.'

George Bishop wrote of the crisis:

'And as for Major Generall Skippon, worthy to bee continually in the best thoughts of truest English: behaved himselfe with that valour and Gallantry, as possibly a man could doe. I heard the General [Fairfax] speak wonderfully to him in his praise, with great expressions. In the first charge he received his wound, shot through the right side under the ribbes, through Armour, and Coat, but not mortall, yet notwithstanding hee kept his Horse, and discharged his place, and would by no means bee drawn off till the Field was wonne; for the space of two hours and a half.'

Bishop attributes the clash on this wing to the desire of the Royalists to take advantage of the wind from the west to blow smoke across the enemy line, but as we have seen the ground itself may have played a part. The shallow re-entrant on Skippon's front would permit the Royalist infantry to advance more quickly and easily than the men to the east and, moreover, the declivity narrowing as they approached the Parliamentary line, the Royalist force would be consolidated into a fearsome wedge, pulling their flanking comrades closer in and concentrating the attack on a narrow front. As Skippon's men tottered and Waller's fell back under the impact, Rupert's cavalry were hastening south in pursuit of that part of the horse they had broken, leaving Ireton's division free to intervene in the infantry contest. Sprigge recounted:

'And the Commissary General seeing one of the enemies Brigades of Foot on his right hand, pressing sore upon our Foot, commanded the Division that was with him, to charge that Body of Foot, and for their better encouragement, he himself with great resolution fell in amongst the Musquetiers, where his horse being shot under him, and himself run through the thigh with a Pike, and into the face with an Halbert, was taken prisoner by the enemy, untill afterwards, when the battell turning, and the enemy in great distraction, he had an happy opportunity to offer his Keeper his liberty, if he would carry him off, which was performed on both parts accordingly.'

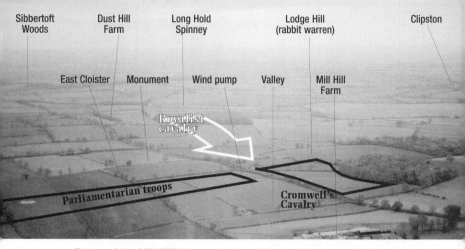

Sibbertoft Woods
Dust Hill Farm
Long Hold Spinney
Lodge Hill (rabbit warren)
Clipston

East Cloister
Monument
Wind pump
Valley
Mill Hill Farm

Royalist cavalry

Parliamentarian troops

Cromwell's Cavalry

Bottom right, Mill Hill Farm and above it Paisnell Spinney with Naseby Covert beyond and Lodge Hill between them. In the middle distance, centre, Long Hold Spinney and Dust Hill Farm to its left; Langdale's position. The cavalry action took place between those positions, east of the modern Naseby to Sibbertoft road which runs diagonally right to left across the view. In the far distance, left, the line of Sibbertoft Woods and, right, beyond Clipston village in the valley, the tree-line of the East Fardon to Great Oxendon road.

All this time Fairfax, on the right wing of his infantry, was scarcely engaged at all. The Parliamentary front line was falling back on the west, but holding firm on the east. Skippon's regiment, in particular, suffered heavily, particulary on its flanks. Foard suggests that Northampton's cavalry hit them from the left and Astley's infantry from the right, a circumstance that accords with the speculation that the re-entrant might have channelled Royalist infantry to smash Waller's men, second from the left, and leave Skippon's exposed on the projecting hilltop to the west. Of the overall situation Sprigge says:

> 'The right hand of the Foot, being the Generals Regiment, stood, being not much pressed upon: Almost all the rest of the main Battail being overpressed, gave ground and went off in some disorder, falling behind the Reserves; But the Colonels and Officers, doing the duty of very gallant Men, in endeavouring to keep their men from disorder, and finding their attempt fruitless therein, fell into the Reserves with their Colours, choosing rather there to fight and die, than to quit the ground they stood on. The Reserves advancing, commanded by Col. Rainsborough, Col. Hammond, and Lieut. col. Pride, repelled the enemy, forcing them to a disorderly retreat. Thus much being said of the Right wing and the main battail, it comes next in order, that an account be given of the Left wing of our Horse.'

What is not clear is what proportion of the Royalist infantry was committed at this time. Given the balance of numbers overall, it would not be unsafe to guess that the second line regiments, Col Paget's of Astley's and Sir John Owen's and maybe Col Gerrat's of Bard's, must have been engaged in order to bring enough pressure to bear to cause the problem. For a while it looked as if the King would have the victory, as Walker observed:

'And had our left Wing but at this time done half so well as either the Foot or right Wing, we had got in a few Minutes a glorious Victory.'

The Cavalry on the East

Rather slower to engage was the left wing of the Royalist horse under Sir Marmaduke Langdale. Their advance took them from the edge of the modern wood, Long Hold Spinney, down into the valley and then up the

Parliamentarian cavalry officer and mounted troopers.

ECWS

steep little hill in the modern field alongside the east edge of the present-day road from Sibbertoft to Naseby. The rabbit warren was in the field beyond to the east. Fairfax's infantry was immediately west of this line, and Langdale's men were thus funnelled into a restricted front. Walker remarked:

> '... our left Wing advanced, consisting of five Bodies of the Northern and Newark Horse; who were opposed by seven great Bodies drawn up to their right Wing by Cromwell who commanded there, and who besides the Advantage of Number had that of the Ground, ours marching up the Hill to encounter them. Yet I needs must say that ours did as well as the Place and their Number would admit; but being flanked and pressed back, they at last gave Ground and fled; Four of the Rebels Bodies close and in good Order followed them, the rest charged our foot.'

Sprigge gives a little more detail:

> '... the Lieutenant-General [Cromwell] not thinking it fit to stand and receive the Enemies charge, advanced forward with ther Right wing of the Horse, in the same order wherein it was placed... Colonel Whaley being the left hand on the right wing, charged first two Divisions of Langdale's Horse, who made a very gallant resistance, and firing at a very close charge, they came to the sword: wherein Col. Whaley's Divisions routed those two Divisions of Langdales, driving them back to Price Rupert's Regiment, being the Reserve of the enemies Foot, whither indeed they fled for shelter, and rallied: the Reserves to Colonel Whaley, were ordered to second him, which they performed with a great deal of resolution.'

That Whalley's men were involved in a heavy action is certain, given their casualties of fifty men, the heaviest amongst Parliamentary cavalry. What is difficult to work out is Walker's reference to Langdale's men being flanked. The lack of shot actually detected on this side of the field sheds doubt on the idea that Fairfax's musketeers opened fire on the charging horse, so the threat must have come from the other side. The abundance of furze or gorse on this side of Turmoore Field and the fear of rabbit holes on the warren hill may have slowed or diverted the horse, exposing their flank to Pye's men coming forward across the warren, or perhaps around the eastern side of it, even if they experienced difficulty. That Pye's were in a serious fight is witnessed by a casualty list of forty-four.

How far back the retreating cavalry were driven is also open to question and the answer lies in the location of the Bluecoats, who began the battle on the left of the reserve. As discussed below, there is reason to believe that they had come no further forward than the southern edge of Dust Hill, west of the modern road which here, in Sibbertoft parish, is in the same place as the road of the time. This leaves an opening on the Royalist's eastern flank through which the rest of the departing cavalry and their pursuers could pass and which would also offer Fairfax a line of attack on the Bluecoats. Sprigge's account continues:

'In the mean time, the rest of the Divisions of the Right wing, being straightened [confined] by Firzes on the right hand, advanced with great difficulty, as also by reason of the unevennesse of the ground, and a Coney-warren over which they were to march, which put them somewhat out of their order, in their advance. Notwithstanding which difficulty, they came up to engaging the residue of the Enemies horse on the left wing, whom they routed, and put into great confusion ... and forced to flee beyond all their Foot, except some that were for a time sheltered by the Brigade of Foot before mentioned.'

An overview of the battlefield looking north east. The Parliamentarian's front line first formed on the dark, ploughed fields north of the barn in the valley north of Mill Hill Farm (bottom right). The Cromwell Monument stands on the near edge of the next, pale, field close to the first big tree in from the Sibbertoft road. That hedge line can be seen to dip before it gets level with the pond on the left. The straight line of the road ceases at the parish boundary and beyond it the field to the left, west, of the road is where the Bluecoats stood. The nearer white building in the distance is on the Kelmarsh to Sibbertoft road. The farthest white building is Lowe Farm and the Royalist baggage was in the area to its left and nearer the camera.

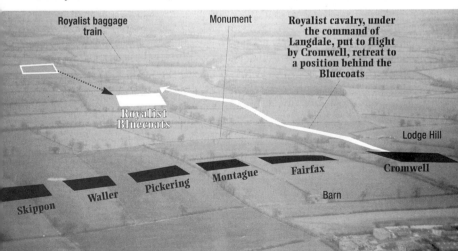

Royalist baggage train

Monument

Royalist cavalry, under the command of Langdale, put to flight by Cromwell, retreat to a position behind the Bluecoats

Royalist Bluecoats

Lodge Hill

Skippon — Waller — Pickering — Montague — Fairfax — Cromwell

Barn

Mill Hill Farm

In short, Cromwell's Ironsides made a thorough job of ejecting the Northern Horse, already reluctant participants, from the field. Not that it was an easy task, as the casualty totals show, and Slingsby, from the Royalist side, puts their brave resistance in context:

'But our Northern horse ... being out front'd & overpour'd by their assailants, after they were close joyn'd, they stood a pritty while, & neither seem'd to yeild, till more came up to their flanks & put ym to rout, & wheeling to our right took ym in disorder, & so presently made our whole horse run ...'

While the fight for the eastern flank was continuing, the disordered cavalry from the west, the Parliamentary left, was pulling itself together. Ireton was out of it, wounded and a prisoner, and Colonel Butler was also wounded. But someone, possibly Fleetwood, rallied the remainder and led them to the right where they took position on Cromwell's former ground, ready to be of service once more.

The Infantry Battle Decided

In the centre Skippon overcame the confusion into which the first Royalist charges had thrown his force and moved his reserves into line, steadily pushing his enemy back, off the hill. The activity of Fairfax at this crucial time is described by Bulstrode Whitelocke, writing from a number of sources in 1682:

'The general had his helmet beat off, and riding in the field bareheaded up and down from one part of his army to another, to see how they stood, and what advantage might be gained, and coming up to his own lifeguard commanded by Colonel Charles D'Oyley [originally the extreme front, right body of cavalry], he was told by him that he exposed himself to too much danger, and the whole army there by ... D'Oyley offered his general his

Opposite page: *A musketeer using a musket rest. He is firing a gun with a matchlock mechanism* (see top this page). *A piece of slow burning rope, known as the match, was held in the grip of the metal device called the serpentine. The trigger released this causing the serpentine to bring the match into contact with the touch-hole where the powder was ignited discharging the weapon. The more reliable flintlock mechanism was also coming into use.*
The cumbersome, heavy armour of the pikeman (right) *began to go out of use during the Civil War period.*

ROYAL ARMOURIES, LEEDS

helmet, but he refused it ... seeing a body of the King's foot stand, and not at all broken, he asked D'Oyley if he had charged that body, who answered, that he had twice charged them, but could not break them.

The identity of this body of infantry is uncertain, but it seems likely that it was Rupert's Bluecoats, holding firm on Dust Hill as the rest of the infantry fell back towards Broadmoor under pressure from the reorganized Parliamentary foot and as their shattered left wing cavalry took shelter behind them. A letter written by a gentleman from Northampton the following day mentions that after the whole Parliamentary army 'did so bestirre them for almost an houre, that they drove all the Kings men from their Ordnance ...' This suggests that the steady advance of the Parliamentary foot must have rolled the Royalists back to Broadmoor past the Parliamentary guns on Cloister before widespread retreat and surrender ensued.

An alternative interpretation is that the Royalists had, while the infantry contested Cloister, brought their guns south to Dust Hill, presumably along the road, and that they were now driven back that far. Cannon balls have been found near Dust Hill Farm, east of the road and, their being no indication of their having been used in action, they may simply have been abandoned as the Parliamentarians advanced.

Given the relief now bestowed on him, Okey saw fit to emerge

Royalists on the left attacking Parliamentarians on the right.   ECWS

from behind his hedges.

'... and presently upon it, God of his providence ordered it so, that our right Wing, which was Colonel Cromwell his Regiment drave the enemy before them; which I perceiving (after one hour's battail) caused all my men to mount and to charge into their Foot, which accordingly they did; and took all their Colours, and 500 Prisoners, besides what wee killed, and all their Armes.'

The Royalist foot were being overwhelmed, as Sprigge confirms:

'To return again to our right wing, which prosecuting their success, by this time had beaten all the enemies horse quite behinde their foot, which when they had accomplished the remaining business was with part to keep the enemies horse from coming to the rescue of their foot, which were now all at mercy, except one Tertia, which with the other part of the horse we endeavoured to break, but could not, they standing with incredible courage & resolution, although we attempted them in the Front, Flanks and Rear, untill such time as the General called up his own Regiment of Foot ... which immediately fell in with them, with But-end of Muskets (the General charging them at the same time with horse) and so broke them.

It was reported in *The Kingdome's Weekly Intelligencer* that:

'The Blue Regiment of the Kings [that is, Rupert's Bluecoats] stood to it very stoutly, and stir'd not, like a wall of brasse, though encompassed by our Forces, so that our men were forced to knock them down with the But end of their Musquets: It is conceived that a great part of them were Irish, and chose rather to die in the field than be hanged.'

Whitelocke continued:

'... Fairfax bid him [D'Oyley] to charge them once again in the front, and that he would take a commanded party, and charge them in the rear at the same time, and they might meet together in the middle ... both charging together put them in confusion, and broke them; and Fairfax and D'Oyley met again in the middle of them, where Fairfax killed the ensign, and one of D'Oyley's troopers took the colours, bragging of the service he had done ... D'Oyley chid the trooper for his boasting and lying, telling him how many witnesses there were who saw the general do it with his own hand; but the general himself bade D'Oyley to let the trooper alone, and said to him, 'I have honour enough, let him take that to himself.'

Rushworth's letter is brief and clear on the point.

'... and then the right wing of our Horse (wherein the Generall was in person) charged in the Flanke of the blew regiment of the Enemies Foot, who stood to it, till the last man, abundance of them slaine, and all the rest surrounded, wounded, and taken these (the hope of their Infantry) being lost Horse and Foot gave backe ...'

These accounts are supported by shot found in the field north of the parish boundary. The boundary runs along the northern edge of the field lying north of the track that leads to Broadmoor Farm. Here the musket balls lay heavy from east to west at the foot of the slope while pistol shot was scattered in a parallel band across the field halfway up towards the track to Prince Rupert's Farm. North of that track there was musket shot once more; a classic pattern of an infantry defence and close-action cavalry attack on foot soldiers from both front and rear, north and south. This, the field alongside the Sibbertoft road, is where the Bluecoats stood 'like a wall of brasse' so heroically.

The great set-piece battle had now come to an end. Popular accounts of the time apparently speak only of abject surrender or outright flight from this stage onwards, but in the light of the finds located by systematic metal detecting, those reports take on quite another meaning; the story was by no means complete.

Chapter 5

THE BATTLE, 14 JUNE 1645 – THE FIGHTING RETREAT

The effective absence of cavalry by the early afternoon left the Royalist foot at the mercy of the better-balanced force. Langdale's men had been thrown off the field, the men around the King stuck to his side and were now falling back with him and Rupert's horse had yet to return from their pursuit of Ireton's wing. The distraction was, it is reported, the baggage.

The Parliamentarian Baggage Train

Quite how long Rupert was gone is hard to guess. South of Red Hill on which they fought the Parliamentary horse, the western end of Cloister, the land falls away, through a little valley with a stream flowing west, to rise once more to Fenny Hill. It then dips before the little clay ridge along which the new A14 runs in a cutting before descending to the shallow valley of the Avon with its two streams.

From the south west the A14 can be seen with a gaggle of white trucks centre left and Naseby village on the extreme right. with the Cold Ashby road running up to it. Between these roads the straight line of Carvell's Lane comes from right to left. The Welford road crosses the A14 near the trucks and the Sibbertoft road bridge is right of that. To the right and beyond is the dark ploughed area of Gibbs Hill stretching as far as the Clipston road.

The position of the Parliamentarian baggage train is open to argument, but could have been positioned south of Naseby village.

Fenny Hill   **Battlefield**   A14   Mill Hill Farm   Carvell's Lane   Gibbs Hill   Naseby village

A detail from Streeter's depiction of the battle formations, showing the Parliamentarian artillery train apparently south of Fenny Hill.

Just where in this undulating landscape the baggage train was situated is not known. The firefight that took place involved mainly outgoing musketry from the defenders, so shotfall would be very scattered. Only disciplined guesswork and visual evidence from the documents remain.

Streeter shows the train in some detail, defended with flintlocks because of the gunpowder present. His engraving of this sector is something of a mess. There are some vague indications of roads and an almost inexplicable shaded area which suggests that his on-the-ground notes were inadequate once back in the studio; perhaps it was intended to indicate the abrupt fall of the land immediately west of Naseby village. What is very clear is the ridge and furrow of Leane Lease Hill which Foard has shown (Figure 49, *Naseby: The Decisive Campaign*) lay alongside the modern Welford road on the southern side and which can also be seen on aerial photographs. This therefore locates the train on the northern side of that road, provided we have confidence in Streeter. Working clockwise from that, the hill immediately north-west of the train is marked Fenny Hill. Then a road from the north-west of Naseby passes on the north or east of the train. De Gomme also shows the train on the flank of Fenny Hill.

The position of the train was a matter discussed between Edward

106

Fitzgerald and Thomas Carlyle to whom the former wrote on 23 September 1842 about a map he had found in the possession of the Vicar. On it he had seen a field he identified as Lean Leys, saying:

'... (I suppose leys or leys of grass – as people now talk of clover-lays, etcc., and these "leys" are lean enough, as I can testify, of a coarse grass and marshy) is a slightly rising pasture that marches to the hill on which the village is built to the west: which hill (wonderful to say) has no name in particular, and so may be called Lean Leys Hill.'

This is accompanied by a sketch map showing the field as being alongside the Cold Ashby road and coming around the west of the village to a line a little to the north of 'Old Welford Road – now leading nowhere', that is, Carvell's Lane as it is called today. This lane was already the straight, ruled-line road of the post-enclosure period. The supposed location of Lean Leys Hill is not marked on the sketch. The post-enclosure field names include, south of Carvell's Lane and adjacent to the enclosure road's end near the village, Lane Leys, Jane Leys, Far Lane Leys and Far Jane Leys, the latter almost reaching the Cold Ashby road to the south. However, the evidence of field names closer to the battlefield itself shows that, when compared with the 1630 map, the actual locations are sometimes very different. The road at the bottom left of Streeter's picture is very probably what became Carvell's Lane across which the area of coarse grass and marsh mentioned by Fitzgerald stretched. Where he would have put the hill is unclear, but the best bet seems to be on rising ground north-west of the village, close to the line of the Welford road. No archaeological evidence was found on the route of the new A14, so perhaps the train was north of the little stream that runs south of Mill Hill and Fenny Hill and on the flank of the latter. The trouble with that area is that the clay soil even today, after modern drainage, is quickly rendered impassable by rain and after the downpours of that week in June 1645 would most certainly have been unsuitable.

As discussed above when considering the approach of the armies to the eventual battleground, no one knew beforehand where the fight was to take place. The heavy, wheeled carts coming from Guilsborough would have kept to the ridge roads entering the village at the south and the expectation was to continue to the north east, bringing the train to the outskirts of the village near the windmill, now the site of the obelisk, or leaving it near the entrance of the village on the flat area astride the Thornby road. The move to the west to take position overlooking Broadmoor could encourage a

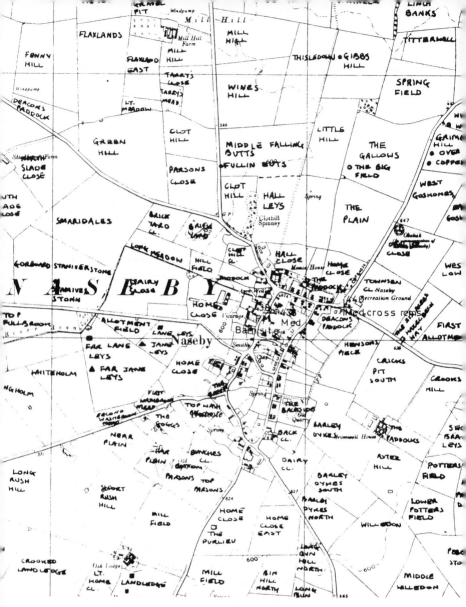

Detail from the field names map of Naseby entered on a mid- 20th century map without the A14 on it. Fenny Hill field is top left, the Obelisk centre right, Mill Field bottom centre and Carvell's Lane runs left from the village with a number of Leys fields below it. An aerial photograph in the Cambridge University Collection, taken in 1947, shows ridge and furrow in the fields named Staniverstone and Smaridales between Carvell's Lane and the Welford road to the north, which some have equated with the ridge and furrow Streeter shows as Leane Leys. M WESTAWAY COLLECTION, CROWN COPYRIGHT

matching move of the train, establishing it either on the ridge now bisected by the A14 or, and for convenience of swift resupply of the artillery, on the southern flank of Fenny Hill, west of the modern Mill Hill Farm, but, as noted above, that brings it into the mud. As to the allocation of troops, the documentary evidence relates to the initial formations and does not give details of who was where after two hours of fighting. In addition to Pride's regiment as a reserve, Streeter shows a smaller unit further back as being a rearguard from the same unit. We have no further information on this body in later fighting, but it might be that Rupert ran into both a guarded baggage train and a defended artillery train as he returned to the battlefield, and suffered delay as a result.

The accounts of the doings of the Royalist right wing during its absence from the main field of battle are vague. Wogan, the Parliamentary commentator who was present at the battle, remarks:

'The King's horse fell a plundering our waggons and gave us time to rally: but a great many of our horse went clear away to Northampton and never could be stopt. The King's right wing, seeing their left wing of horse beat in, marched back again the same way they came.'

This is shaky reporting. Wogan could not have witnessed the wagon plundering, nor could Rupert have observed events relating to their left wing from a position closer to the village, but Wogan could well have observed the return of Rupert's horse along the western side of the battlefield. If part of Ireton's horse fled to Northampton they would have gone back flanking the village and bearing left to the ridge route and sound ground, avoiding Fitzgerald's marshy pasture. A force in pursuit might have happened on baggage wagons south of the village, less well defended, and lost time seeking plunder, only encountering the artillery train on their return.

The Reverend John Mastin, writing a history of his parish of Naseby in 1792, recorded that burials had been found near the site of the windmill, but by this he meant the more recent structure in the second field south of the village and east of the Thornby road, Mill Field, opposite the entrance to the modern Oak Farm. That windmill, too, has now gone, but from this place the views to Northampton, towards Market Harborough and towards the eventual battlefield are clear, in which case there was no need to move the train when the armies moved to the west.

Rushworth, Fairfax's secretary, wrote from Market Harborough on 15 June, saying, with a vividness that suggests he might have

This is Mastin's windmill (page 109) that once stood in Mill Field, south of Naseby on the Thornby road. It is possible that the Parliamentarian baggage train was sited at this location for the battle. M WESTAWAY COLLECTION

witnessed the event:

'A party of theirs that broke through the left wing of Horse, came behind the rear to our traine, the leader of them being a person somewhat in habit [clothing] like the Generall, in a red Mountero, as the Generall had, he came as a friend; our Commander of the guard of the Traine went with his hat in his hande, and asked him how the day went, thinking it had been the Generall; the Cavelier whom we since heard was Rupert, asked him and the rest, if they would have quarter [would surrender], they cryed no, Gave fire and instantly beat them off.'

The fight may not have been as brief as Rushworth implies; indeed, given that the defenders suffered nine casualties against cavalry, it might have been quite a nasty business. Furthermore Pride's men may have taken a hand. The original idea of taking the train and the supplies of gunpowder that might otherwise refresh the Parliamentary artillery, to say nothing of the musketeers, probably seemed a good one, particularly as things had seemed to be going well for the King when Rupert last saw the battle. All this, action and location, are in the realm of conjecture and readers can offer opinion of equal weight until archaeological evidence settles the matter. What is clear is that on the eventual return of the Royalist horse the fight was back on Dust Hill and even that phase may have been over. Rupert could do nothing other than hasten to find the King.

The Retreat to the Royal Baggage

If the location of the Parliamentarian baggage is conjectural, the Royalist train can be placed with much greater certainty, as can the events that marked the retreat towards it. Across Broadmoor a scattering of musket balls has been found, forming two distinct bands running back to the parish boundary at the foot of Dust Hill, evidence either of the action of the Parliamentary 'Forlorn Hope' or of retreating Royalists. On the hillside to the north there is an arc of shot on the west which appears to be that resulting from Okey's action earlier in the day as recounted above. On the east are the bands of musket shot and scattering of pistol balls we associate with the defiant stand of Rupert's Bluecoats. Nothing else of significance has been found on this slope. A picture forms of men retreating from Cloister, a hedgehog of pikemen covering their musketeers who are firing to discourage their pursuers, perhaps dragoons attacking from Sulby Hedges, but this is conjecture.

Edward Wogan, who was with Okey's Dragoons, recounted:

'But seeing all their horse beaten out of the field, and surrounded with our horse and foot, they [the Royalists] laid down their arms with condition not to be plundered. Presently a noise was spread among our horse, that no man must light [dismount] to plunder on pain of death, and forthwith to follow the King's horse; which accordingly we did, but very leisurely, being much discontented to leave all the plunder of the field to the foot.'

The pause in activity and the gap in finds of shot on the ground thus appear to be caused by the willingness of exhausted and unsupported infantry to surrender, and the prisoners taken that day were many, some four thousand. Sprigge sheds further light.

'The Generall ... seeing ... our whole Army (saving some Bodies of horse which faced the enemy) being busied in the execution upon the foot, and taking, and securing prisoners, endeavouring to put the Army again into as good order as they could receive, to the perfecting of the work that remained: Our foot were somewhat more than a quarter of a mile behinde the horse, and although there wanted no courage nor resolution in the horse themselves alone to have charged the enemy ... It was

The Sibbertoft road meanders north past Dust Hill Farm (bottom centre) to its junction with the Kelmarsh road coming up from the right. The footpath continues north to the Sibbertoft-Clipston road on which Lowe Farm stands on the right. The Royalist baggage train was probably halted on the near side of the large rectangular field left, west, of the farm.

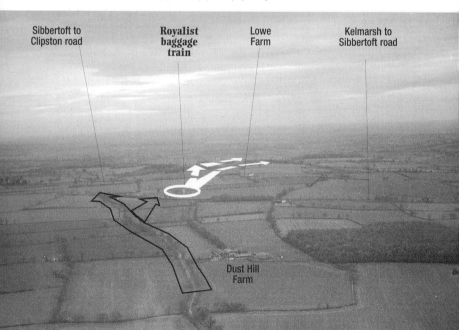

Sibbertoft to Clipston road

Royalist baggage train

Lowe Farm

Kelmarsh to Sibbertoft road

Dust Hill Farm

ordered our horse should not charge the enemy untill the foot were come up ...'

What confuses the account is that the time and place of this activity and decision-making is compressed; the finds of shot make that quite clear. The modern roads in Sibbertoft parish are virtually identical with those of 1645 and walking north, that is, retreating in the footsteps of the Royalists, small concentrations of shot have been found alongside the road in the field to the west, each suggesting another brief, brave stand to slow the Parliamentary advance. Just short of the Kelmarsh to Sibbertoft road which comes up from the east, the musket balls lay thick in the field on the eastern edge of the Naseby road, perhaps directed at cavalry on that road by men making for the baggage train to the north-east, between the Clipston and Kelmarsh roads.

The Royalist artillery and baggage had had to make its way from East Farndon by an indirect route as the hills and sodden fields on the direct line would most certainly have made the carriages and waggons bog down. The road still goes down from the Farndon-Oxendon ridge to Clipston, turning west on the northern edge of the village and making its way up the hill to the Sibbertoft plateau through the narrows of the closes of old Nobold and the field on the opposite side of the road to the north, a journey of about three miles. This would take over an hour for the leading vehicles which would have been arriving as the battle started and the last of them would still be coming up as the retreat took place. Streeter shows the Royalist train coming up to Sibbertoft from the east while the Parliamentary baggage is already safely laagered. As a result of the slow progress of the back markers, the road to Clipston was blocked to outgoing traffic.

Immediately north of the junction of the Kelmarsh and Naseby roads south of Sibbertoft a footpath strikes north to the Sibbertoft to Clipston road, possibly the continuation of the Naseby road towards the site of the castle north east of the village. In a band to the east of that path, in an arc that curves within the visible hedge line, a heavy concentration of shot indicates a fierce battle, suggesting that the guards of the train and the musketeers who had retreated to it defended themselves with vigour from a position immediately south west of Lowe Farm. Some of the shot is of a larger calibre than musket shot and came, perhaps, from swivel guns mounted on the wagons of the baggage train. This location for the baggage is supported by the discovery of a hoard of silver coins that was buried here. Slingsby wrote:

'... they being horse & foot in good order, & we but a few horse only, & those mightily discourag'd; yt so we were immediately made to run, & ye enemy in pursuit of us gain'd bag and baggage all we had, wch they found to be very rich pillage: & tho' our Waggons were left at a good distance yet could they not be carry'd off, but some were taken, & some overthrown & monys shaken out, wch made our soulgiers to venture their lives once more, wch was but to stay and take it up.'

The Last Stand

The indications of continuing fighting were then found along the Sibbertoft to Clipston road and on Moot Hill and Wadborough Hill to the north of that road, fighting to which a number of journal entries may refer. It is clear that precision in describing time and location is largely lacking from contemporary reports, but repairing the deficiency is not a precise activity either. In this account the finds of shot are given prime consideration.

East of the point at which the footpath reaches the Clipston road shot lies on both sides of the lane and, in the field beyond, a trail of shot leads north down the western side of the field into the gully or

Looking north from the Sibbertoft-Clipston road, the top of a pointed Wellingtonia tree (right of the signpost) marks Castle Yard and Hellcombe is left of that. To the right the spinney, fenced in pale materials.

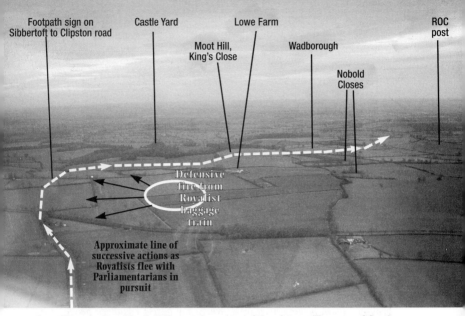

Footpath sign on Sibbertoft to Clipston road
Castle Yard
Lowe Farm
ROC post
Moot Hill, King's Close
Wadborough
Nobold Closes
Defensive fire from Royalist baggage train
Approximate line of successive actions as Royalists flee with Parliamentarians in pursuit

Lowe Farm is the white building at the centre of the picture. The cone of Castle Yard, the motte and bailey, shows to the left in Sibbertoft Wood. To the right of Lowe Farm the hedges of the Nobold closes straddle the Clipston road. Above the farm a lone tree stands on the near edge of King's Close and a footpath passes it, turns right down the hedge and then away from the camera in the valley between Moot Hill, left, and Wadborough on the right.

coombe that passes west of the motte and bailey, known as Castle Yard. This gully is Hellcombe, the way to Marston Trussell, and the alleged location of Cavalier burials. Another trail of shot runs from the road across the field a little further to the east, passing just south of a hill-top spinney and onto the top of Moot Hill, now marked with an Ordnance Survey triangulation pillar at 188m, west of which a thicker cluster was found. The trail then continues to the north east, down into the narrow valley between Moot Hill and Wadborough Hill. On the side of Moot Hill the finds consisted entirely of pistol balls. In the hollow some of the most concentrated fire on the whole battlefield was found, equal in density on both sides of the little valley. A few balls were on the top of Wadborough, but none on the southern slope. The trace of battle then staggers east, off the hill and to the eastern side of what is now a tree-filled gully overlooked from the single-track Clipston to Marston Trussell road curving north and westwards towards the River Welland. This remarkable series of finds doubtless tells the story of the final phase of the fight, so how might we interpret it?

The shot on the Clipston road east of the footpath must be another

Parish boundary

Wadborough

Area where
large finds of
shot have been
found

Parliamentarian view of the Royalists' last stand on Wadborough, from the edge of King's Close looking north east. Where the parish boundary hedge in the valley passes the wood on the left the large finds of shot were made.

attempt by the Royalists of the baggage train to hold off Parliamentarians sweeping around them clockwise. By now Fairfax had, presumably, managed to gather together his foot and his horse into a properly drawn battle formation. Driven back from the road, part of the Royalist infantry and horse made off due north down Hellcombe, peppered with musketry as they went and pursued by the horse. Many of them, however, made for the hill on which, earlier, they had seen the King's standard flying, Moot Hill, the field that was later known as King's Close. Their resistance here was soon broken and as they fled down into the steep-sided little valley where they were followed and pistolled by cavalry. They managed to gain the flank of Wadborough and there they reformed, turned and subjected their enemy to fierce fire. The Parliamentarian force was certainly fully reconstituted as an army of infantry and cavalry by this time. Perhaps that was the first unsuccessful attempt, and Wadborough the second victorious attack that Sprigge speaks of:

'It was ordered our horse should not charge untill the foot were come up; for by this time our foot that were disordered upon the first Charge, being in shorter time than is well imaginable, rallyed again, were comming up upon a fast march to joyn with our horse, who were again put in two wings, within Carbine shot of the enemy, leaving a wide space for the battail of foot to fall in, whereby there was framed, as it were in a trice, a second good Batalia at the latter end of the day; which the enemy perceiving, and that if they stood, they must expect a second Charge from our Horse, Foot and Artillery (they having lost all their Foot and Guns before) and our Dragoons having already begun to fire upon their horse, they not willing to abide a second shock upon so great a disadvantage as this was like to be, immediately ran away ...'

Given the concentration of shot to the west of Wadborough, there is little doubt that this is the hill on which the unknown gentleman of Northampton wrote that the bodies lay 'the most thick on the hill the Kings men stood on.' But one of the puzzles of Wadborough is the lack of shot on the southern face of the hill. Perhaps there is a clue in Sprigge. Evidently time was taken to reform both armies; a pause in the relentless pressure of battle to catch the breath, load the musket, wipe the sweat from the face and dry the palms of the hands. If Fairfax reformed his battle south of the hill, looking up the gentle slope to the shaken remnants of his enemy, there may well have been a moment of silence before the King's men turned and ran back for Harborough, the way they had come. Rushworth's account is characteristically concise, unfortunately.

'... but still our Horse, though one would have beaten ten, (such a feare was the Enemy possessed with all) would not pursue in heate but take the Foot to flank them, the King cryed out, face about once and give one charge and recover the day, our Men Horse and Foot came on with that courage, that before ever wee gave fire they faced about and ran cleere away, and happy was he that was best mounted ...'

Another possibility has been identified in the pattern of drainage here. The Nobold enclosure north of the road, Englands, was a field adjacent to the village on the south side. The most likely use of such an enclosed field was the safekeeping of livestock. A little stream runs down towards the road along the north-eastern side of the field and beyond it a gentle slope rises to Wadborough. Livestock need drinking water and it seems possible that either the stream had been deepened or even used as a pond feed, or that drinking beasts had, in the persistently rainy weather, created a quagmire. Either would have been an impediment to attack from this place and thus the reason for absence of shot. Finally, it is possible that this flank was the intended line of Fairfax's cavalry's last attack and thus, like Red Hill and Lodge Hill, free of shot.

And what of the King and Prince Rupert? Their infantry had

resisted doggedly during their retreat from the Clipston road and over Moot Hill to Wadborough. It may be that it was in this period that the incidents reported by Sir Edward Walker took place. He recounts the start of the cavalry pursuit of the Royalist foot shortly after Cromwell's wing had broken Langdale's horse, saying:

'Four of the Rebels Bodies close and in good order followed them [Langdale's], the rest charged our foot. At this instant the King's Horse-guards and the King at the Head of them were ready to charge those who followed ours ...'

This is usually interpreted as taking place on Dust Hill, but the subsequent events accord more closely with the traces on the ground further north. If one takes the following proposed intervention as being near Moot Hill, viewed by the king and his companions from the hill carrying the Clipston to Marston Trussel road, an alternative narrative emerges.

'... when a Person of Quality, 'tis said the Earl of Carnwath, took the King's Horse by the Bridle, turned him about, swearing at Him and saying, Will you go upon your death? and at the same time the Word being given, March to the right Hand (which was both from assisting ours or assailing them, and (as most concluded) was a civil Command for every one to shift for himself) we turned about and ran upon the Spur for almost quarter of a Mile, and then the Word being given to make a Stand, we did so; though the Body could never be rallyed. Those that came back made a Charge, wherein some of them fell. By this time Prince Rupert was come with a good Body of Horse from the right Wing; but they having done their part, and not being in Order, could never be brought to charge again, nor to rally any of the broken Troops...'

Rushworth confirms, from the opposing side, that a final charge was made by the King's cavalry, and the combination of the failure to support the foot and this last, desperate and futile attack by the horse can be visualized as relating to the infantry's final efforts on Wadborough. Okey, too, claims a hand in the final flurry.

'After this the King his Horse drew up into a body againe: and then I drew up my Dragoons, and charged the King's Regiment of Horse, and they faced about and run away and never made any stay till they came to Leicester ...'

From the World War II Observer Corps post, a raised and walled platform in brick just off the summit of the north-running one-track lane from Clipston to Marston Trussell, the land falls away to the north west in front of the observer towards the tree-filled gully around which the last of the infantry fled. Perhaps it was there that this last burst of cavalry action took place and from this height that Charles I witnessed the final defeat.

The Flight

The attempts to evade capture or death had long been in progress. The Royalist baggage train included not only supplies but followers of greater or less respectability. As Cromwell's reserves of horse chased Langdale's men north waggons were still pushing up the hill from Clipston, clogging the narrow lane through the old Nobold enclosures and preventing retreat. Those on foot could veer northwards, but with Moot Hill and Wadborough being a battleground, the only way would seem to be through the enclosed field of Nobold, Englands or Inlands, just north of the road along the west side of which the modern parish boundary runs, just as it did at the time. The contemporary accounts of what took place range from the critical to the positively gleeful. The letter from the Gentleman of Northampton known as *A more exact and perfect Relation of the great*

From the Clipston to Marston Trussell road, which becomes Dick's Hill further on, a view can be had of Wadborough and of Sibbertoft Wood, in the distance to the left. In the valley below, to the right, trees fill a steep gully. Shot was found running around the near side of this obstacle; perhaps the final fight of the battle viewed from this position by the King.

Wadborough Sibbertoft Wood Tree-filled gully

Likely location
from where
King Charles
viewed the
retreat of his
forces

From the hedge on the south side of King's Close the field alongside the Clipston road, Englands, can be seen. It hooks to the left beyond the power line pole and along the far hedge coins were found. Possibly the scene of the plunder and assault on the women.

victory written on 15 June says:

'... there was many of the Wagons taken with rich plunder, and others with Arms and Ammunition, about 50 loads of Muskets, Pikes, Match and Bullets, abundance of Trunks, which the Souldiers soone emptied, as they did the Wagons that carried the middle sort of Ammunition Whoores, whoe were full of money and rich apparell, there being about 1500 of that tribe, the gentler sort in Coaches, whereof I only saw 7 Coaches with Horses taken stuffed with commodity, and the common rabble of common vermin of foot, 500 of them at least being taken and kept within guard, until order was taken to dispose of them and their mates, many of these Irish women, of cruel countenances, some of them were cut by our Souldiers when they tooke them.'

Rushworth told of the killing that took place.

'... the Irish women Prince Rupert brought upon the field (wives of the bloody Rebels in Ireland his Majesties dearly beloved subjects) our souldiers would grant no quarter too, about 100 slain of them, and most of the rest of the whores that attended that wicked Army are marked in the face or nose, with a slash or cut.'

The finds in Englands are of coins, pathetic relics of the plunder and slaughter of the Royalist followers. Nichols, in his late 18th-century history of Leicestershire, repeated a story said to have been related by an eye-witness.

'In the south part of Farndon-field, within the gate-place in the road between Naseby and Farndon, the Parliament horse galloping along, as Mr Morton (the author of the *Natural*

120

History of Northamptonshire) was informed by an eye witness, cut and slashed the women, with this sarcasm at every stroke, "Remember Cornwall, you Whores!" Sir Ralph Hopton, as they said, having used their women in Cornwall in the like manner.'

This has been taken to mean that the incident took place close to the area in which Rupert first drew up his force at the start of the day. However, there is no road as such between Naseby and Farndon and the passage makes better sense if 'road' is understood as 'route' and the gate-place is identified as the access from the enclosed field of Englands to the open fields to the east, south of Farndon.

The tendency was to flee downhill and away by much the same route as they had come. Slingsby recalled:

'The way I took was upon my right hand, leaving Harborrow on my left, only Leif. Coll, Atkinson & 3 more following me, wn all besides took Harborrow on ye right & were come to Leister long before we got thither.'

Some are said to have been caught in Marston Trussell, having rushed straight down from Sibbertoft and across the flood plain to the river and into the village. The roads were changed in the 1870s

Bandolier with charges, each containing a pre-measured quantity of black powder; also a bag for carrying musket balls. ROYAL ARMOURIES LEEDS

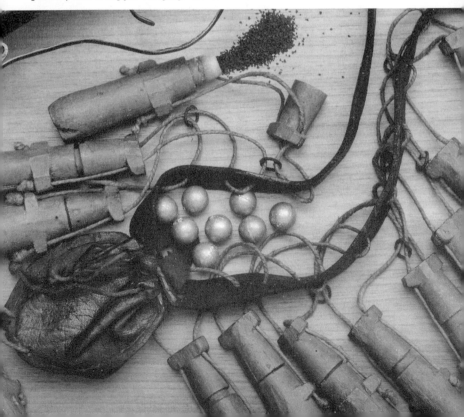

The view south of south east from Dick's Hill. On the right are the steep hills north of Sibbertoft and the narrow, wooded valley of Hellcombe. The Sibbertoft to Marston Trussell road is a short way behind the camera.

Hellcombe
Dick's Hill, road to Clipston
Royalists route away from the battlefield

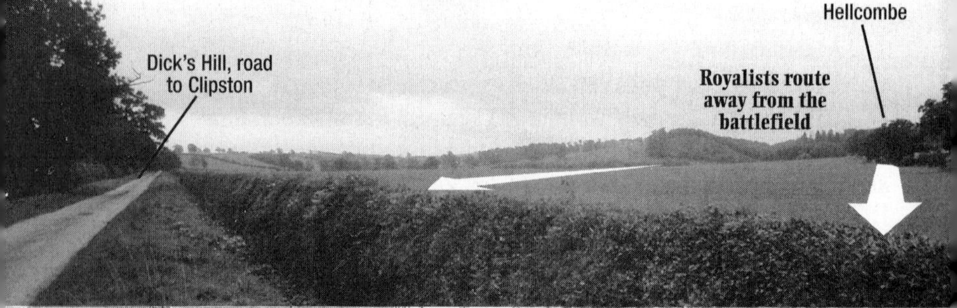

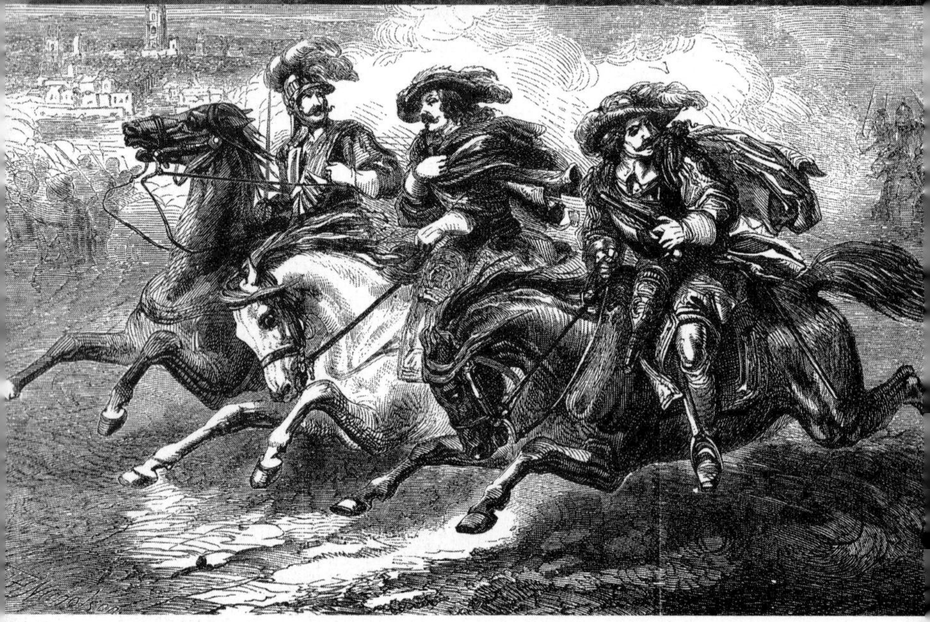

Royalists flee the field at Naseby.

when the lake was made to enhance the park of the newly built Marston Trussell Hall. In 1645 the Sibbertoft road entered further west and the Lubenham road left the main street along the line of the north-running bridleway to turn east along a back lane behind the houses and gardens. What seemed to be the main road ran as far as the church and the manor house next to the site of the former, moated, manor-house. This street was a dead-end, literally, for those cavaliers caught here by the pursuing New Model Army. Edward Fitzgerald wrote to Thomas Carlyle on 30 September 1842 about his investigation of the incident.

'I then went on to Marston itself: which has a story to tell.

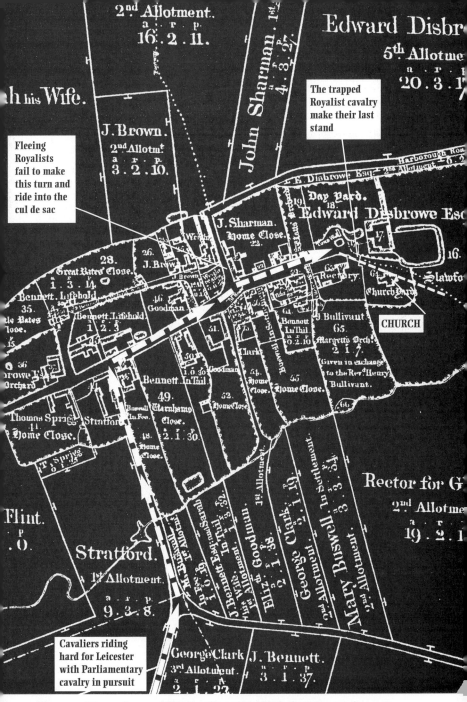

Fleeing Royalists fail to make this turn and ride into the cul de sac

The trapped Royalist cavalry make their last stand

CHURCH

Cavaliers riding hard for Leicester with Parliamentary cavalry in pursuit

The map of the enclosure of Marston Trussell in 1815. To make way for a new Hall, a park and a lake on the west, the road from the south was re-routed further east, approximately through the land marked Watchman's Close, 49. Here the old road can be seen turning right into the main street but then left and right again to Market Harborough. Fleeing Royalists failed to turn left and were caught by the church. NORTHAMPTONSHIRE RECORD OFFICE 2867B

The Royalists fled, and were pursued thither, and a great slaughter made. And I, without having heard the story, found myself entrapped in my progress exactly as they were. I drove my gig into Marston, straight along the road from Sibbertoft, to the Church: where, at the very church yard gate, the road stopped: went no farther. Had a fellow with a drawn sword been behind me, I must have turned and stood at bay, or received an inglorious wound. And in this plight exactly the Royalists found themselves. This end of the town is called, and has always been called Pudding-bay-end [Pudding-bag-end in local usage] – it is a 'cul-de-sac': and was much more so 200 years ago ... So here the Royalists stood at bay, and there was a grand scrimmage: so that a little paddock just under the Church yard is called Slaughford: which the parson told me meant Slaughter ford... As to proofs of the slaughter, my parson's father was digging in the churchyard many years ago to found a vault for his own family: and he came upon a heap of decayed bodies (just like that I lit upon) in the very place where tradition has always pointed out the grave of the slaughtered to be, and which was marked by that sinking in of the ground, which always follows

Slawford field where the Cavaliers made their last stand. It seems equally likely that fleeing Royalist infantry, using the footpath from Clipston, also ended up in this location and met their deaths. See text page 150.

Footpath from
Marston Trussell
to Clipston

Marston Trussell Church. This doorway, with its shaped oak timbers, dates from the 14th century and so 'witnessed' the fighting in the churchyard. Local tradition has it that the 'last stand' was made in the meadow by the church, (later to be known as [Slawford] Slaughterford). Groups of Royalists from that last stand sought refuge in the church but were stopped by the church gate where they were cut down. In the churchyard, gravepits have been found where the skeletons were laid in various positions, indicating a hasty, shallow burial. One portion of the graveyard, where the ground had sunk, was once known as the "Cavaliers' Grave". Also two cannon balls were dug up in the vicinity, one of which was purported to have been shot clean through the building. The path past the porch is a public footpath which leaves the churchyard by a stile into the Slaughterford field.

a heap of bodies buried shallowly.'

The King himself made for Market Harborough. From the summit of the road behind Wadborough, from which he was dissuaded from charging to the aid of his infantry, the natural line of march lies between Thorpe Lubenham to the left and East Farndon's hills to the east, back through the ford over which he passed that morning; Bloodyman's Ford. Here, according to *The Moderate Intelligencer*, a parliamentary publication, he was almost caught.

> '... the King himself in person being necessitated, with his own troop only, to charge through the body for his escape and it is said that his flight was aided by a gentleman of the Bedchamber, that stood next the King, and cryed, hold your hands the King will yield his person, which while they did, hee got away, and so escaped.'

The details of the flight are not plentiful or reliable. It was said that the saddles now at Wistow Hall, near Leicester, are those of the King and Prince Rupert, left on the horses they changed here on their precipitate journey, though they do not look suitable for combat. Edward Wogan's opinion of the pursuit was scarcely triumphal.

> 'Certainly if there had been but 1,000 of the King's horse

On the East Farndon road, leaving Market Harborough next to Welland Park, a bridge, right, has replaced Bloodyman's Ford.

Bridge that later was built across the stream next to the fording place

Bloodyman's Ford

King Charles was almost caught at this point

rallied, and charged us in our disorderly and discontente
pursuit, they might without doubt have beaten back again, an
routed our foot which was richly laden with plunder and coul
by no means be brought together in a long time.

'We leisurely continued the pursuit till we came within 2
miles of Leicester, where we found part of the King's horse
drawn up; but they never offered to charge us, not we them, but
we stood and looked at each other till night came on. They
marched into Leicester, and we were called back again.'

Casualties

The destruction of the King's army had been comprehensive. Few
infantry were left and losses among the horse must have been
serious. Sir Edward Walker wrote:

'... and so after all the endeavours of the King and Prince
Rupert, to the hazard of their Persons, they were fain to quit the
Field, and to leave Fairfax Master of all our Foot, Cannon,
Baggage and Plunder taken at Leicester. Our Foot had Quarter
given to them, but all were Prisoners, except some few Officers
who escaped, and our Horse made haste, never staying until
they came under the Works of Leicester ... The Number slain
that Day is uncertain, those of Quality slain of the King's Army
were Sir Thomas Dalizon, Sir Richard Cave, Sir Peter Browne,
Collonel Thomas, Lieutenant Collonel Davies, and above 100
Officers and Gentlemen out of the Northern and Newark Horse
and Prince Rupert's Troops. In the Pursuit of the Rebels,
cruelly killed above 100 Weomen and Souldiers Wives, and
some of them of Quality ...'

The officers of foot who escaped probably did so because they were
mounted. From the Parliamentarian point of view Sprigge reported:

'The number of the slain we had not a certain account of by
reason of the prosecution of our Victory, and speedy advance to
the reducing of Leicester; the prisoners taken in the field were
about five thousand, whereof were six Colonels, eight Lieut.
Colonels, eighteen Majors, seventy Captains, eighty
Lieutenants, eighty Ensignes, two hundred other inferior
Officers, besides the Kings Footmen, and household servants,
the rest common Souldiers, four thousand five hundred. The
enemy lost very gallant men, and indeed their foot,
commanded by Lord Astley, were not wanting in courage...'

'Their Train of Artillery was taken, all their Ordnance,

(being brasse Guns) where of two were Demi-Canon, besides two Morter-pieces, (the enemy got away not one Carriage) eight thousand Arms and more, forty Barrels of powder, two hundred horse, with their riders ...'

From this it also appears that the officers who escaped were in the minority and that there was no general abandonment of the men. John Rushworth, as secretary to Fairfax, was in a position to give authoritative evidence but his estimates vary markedly from the others.

'I viewed the dead bodies, from the Battell to Harborough truly I estimate them not to be above 700, together with those slaine in the fields running away, but in pursuit between Harborough and Leicester, and by townes, conceived about 300 more slaine, abundance wounded ...'

If these figures are taken together with his estimate of prisoners at 3,000 the total of killed and captured comes to 4,000 while others take that figure for the prisoners alone. As to numbers, Colonel Okey reports much the same as Sprigge and there seems little basis for contesting their figures. They relate reasonably to the initial strengths, especially when the number of killed is taken into account. The 'Gentleman of Northampton' said that:

'The bodies lay slaine about four miles in length, the most thick on the hill the Kings men stood on. I cannot think there was few lesse than four hundred men slaine, and truly I think not many more, and neere 300 horses. Wee tooke at least four thousand Prisoners on the ground between Naseby and Harborough, neere three hundred Carriages, whereof twelve of them were Ordnance, one drawn by twenty six Horses, carrying a twenty four pound bullet ...'

The narrative accounts say little of Parliamentarian losses, other than the deaths of a few prominent persons. Glenn Foard, however, has unearthed a detailed account for payments made in respect of the care of the wounded in Northampton which he gives as Appendix 3 in his book and from this a casualty report of a kind can be constructed. The left wing of cavalry suffered 136 wounded, the right wing 129 and the foot 258. This total of 535 includes forty-five who eventually died. In their letter of the same day, 14 June 1645, to the Speaker of the House of Commons Harcourt Leighton and Thomas Herbert, Parliamentary Commissioners with the army, wrote that their losses had not exceeded 200 slain. It thus appears that the killed amounted to fewer than 700 in all. The King's Oxford Army was, however, destroyed and with it went all realistic hope of eventual victory in this war.

The Political Price

The defeat at Naseby was more than a military disaster. The political consequences were substantial. In his flight the king's private papers were left behind and fell into the hands of his enemies, exposing his private correspondence with his queen and others during the previous eighteen months. The plans to use soldiers from Ireland and from the continent of Europe and the tolerance of, or even promotion of, Roman Catholicism were publicized in a book of the letters published by order of Parliament later in 1645.

James Butler, Earl of Ormonde, was appointed by Charles I to oppose the Irish rebellion in 1641. In a letter dated 15 December 1644 Charles wrote to him:

'... I doe hereby promise them, (and command you to see it done) that the Penall Statutes against Roman Catholiques shall not be put in execution, the Peace being made, and they remaining in their due obedience; and further, that when the Irish gives me that assistance which they have promised, for the suppression of this Rebellion [i.e. that of the English Parliament], and I shall be restored to my Rights, then I will consent to the Repeal of them by a Law ...'

Another letter discovered in the King's Cabinet was one from a Colonel Fitz-William and was said to have been forwarded to the king by the queen on 16 May 1645. The Colonel proposed to bring an army of ten thousand men and more of the Confederate Catholics to England. So it continues for more than forty pages, building to an aggressive essay peppered with specific references to the text of the letters and ending with a

129

The King's letters are discovered.

damning six point summary of the King's lies, evasions and treacherous plans to use foreign troops against his own people. It was a propaganda coup of massive proportions, putting the final touch to the victory of 14 June.

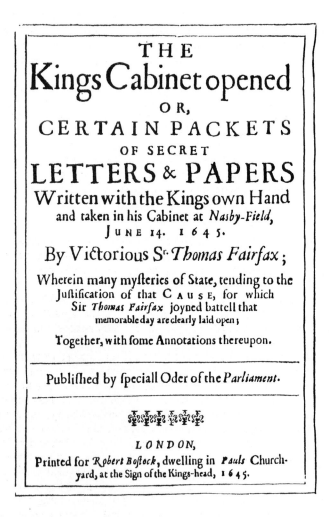

THE
Kings Cabinet opened
OR,
CERTAIN PACKETS
OF SECRET
LETTERS & PAPERS
Written with the Kings own Hand
and taken in his Cabinet at *Nasby-Field*,
JUNE 14. 1645.

By Victorious S. *Thomas Fairfax*;

Wherein many mysteries of State, tending to the Justification of that CAUSE, for which Sir *Thomas Fairfax* joyned battell that memorable day are clearly laid open;

Together, with some Annotations thereupon.

Published by speciall Oder of the *Parliament*.

LONDON,
Printed for *Robert Bostock*, dwelling in *Pauls* Church-yard, at the Sign of the Kings-head, 1645.

The title page of The Kings Cabinet opened, *Charles's secret correspondence.*

Chapter 6

EXPLORING THE GROUND

The territory it is necessary to cover to explore the entire campaign is extensive and requires travel by car or, if the reader is seriously robust, by bicycle. If the events of 14 June alone are to be considered a car is still easiest, bicycle practical and, with some planning after evaluating this chapter, travel on foot like the infantry of the time is possible. The structure of the advice that follows is chronological in style; it follows the sequence of historical events. However, the locations are marked on the sketch map (page 136) and are identified with letter codes so that the visitor can choose where to go, and in what order, to suit their own convenience. Fixed viewpoints answer only some of the challenges of investigating the battle so some of the suggestions here are for routes between viewpoints. The intention is to provide sufficient information to free the visitor to pursue a self-selected route. If time is short, visit viewpoints B, E, H and K.

ACCESS

The campaign area is flanked on the west by the M1 motorway from which, at Junction 15A, the A43 leads to the A45 Northampton to Daventry road which crosses the M1 again at Junction 16. From the north and north west the A14, which runs immediately south of the battlefield, originates from Junction 19, but there is no access at that place for traffic coming from the south on the M1. Further north Junction 20 is with the A4303 to Market Harborough. From the A14 visitors can use the junctions with the A5199 south of Welford or with the A508 at Kelmarsh.

The railways can bring visitors to Market Harborough, Northampton or Rugby. From London St Pancras, Midland Mainline services pass through Market Harborough on their way to Nottingham or Sheffield, and some of them stop here en route, but not those trains on which one can book a bicycle, so cyclists have to take pot luck that there will be room on the train. From London Euston services to Northampton and to Rugby on the way to Birmingham and the north west are provided by Silverlink and by Virgin. Bus services are not so easy to use but, for example and at the time of writing, there is a service during school termtime from Market Harborough's Market Hall to Naseby on Tuesdays and Fridays at 12.15pm, arriving at 12.55pm and a return service at 4.15pm. The journey takes about forty minutes. There is also a full daily service from Northampton to Market Harborough which vigorous walkers could use to access the start and finish points of a twelve-mile walk from Kelmarsh to Naseby and on via Sibbertoft to Great Oxendon. For bus services in this part of Northamptonshire, area 9, check availablity and times by telephoning 0870 6082608. For trains call

08457 484950. Tourist Information Centres can provide further information on transport, car and cycle hire and so forth. Their telephone numbers are as follows: Daventry – 01327 300277. Market Harborough – 01858 821270. Northampton – 01604 622677. Rugby – 01788 534970.

Once in the battlefield area there are relatively few footpaths to give the visitor access to the ground itself and the roads are narrow and ill-provided with parking places. Much of the viewing has to be done by looking over hedges and by walking on roads. As this is countryside consisting of working farms, care must be taken not to trespass on private land, not to open gates and to shut those on public paths, and to park without causing obstruction to roads or to farmers' gateways. Remember that modern farming machinery is huge! Not only does it take up a lot of room, but it is more formidable than a World War II tank and capable of inflicting similar damage on carelessly parked cars or on jaywalkers. Not that the authors have ever encountered anything but a friendly welcome; one just has to respect that those who live here are striving to make a living and not just amusing themselves by playing at gardening on a big scale.

If leaving the car to walk, even the short distance between the lay-by and the Cromwell Monument on the Naseby to Sibbertoft road, be sure to lock it and secure or cover up any valuables. It is not unknown for thieves to target visitors' vehicles.

EQUIPMENT AND REFERENCE MATERIALS

It is possible to enjoy a visit without any material additonal to this book. However, to get the most out of the experience it is suggested that Ordnance Survey maps are taken. For the serious visitor the 1:25,000 Explorer 223 is ideal. This covers the entire area of operations of 14 June 1645 as well as a good deal of the terrain over which the armies approached and departed, from Market Harborough in the north to Northampton in the south. Two of the 1:50,000 Landranger maps are needed if wider coverage but less detailed scale is wanted. Numbers 152 and 141 deal with the southern and northern sectors respectively. An ordinary road atlas will answer the rest of the traveller's needs. Some Ordnance Survey Grid references have been included in the text for the convenience of those who have one of these maps and for those unfamiliar with how they work an explantion will be found on the map itself.

People intending to walk the footpaths should be aware that even a little rain makes a lot of mud around here and walking boots or rubber boots are needed. In addition a compass will be useful for orientation, although the battle area is not hard to understand as the Naseby to Sibbertoft road runs virtually south to north and the Clipston to East Fardon road is almost parallel to it. Wide open country is a feature of north Northamptonshire and it is possible to see a very long way, given reasonably clear weather. A pair of field glasses or binoculars will be useful to identify features at a distance.

LANDMARKS

There are a number of features that can be recognised from afar and visitors are recommended to take a good look when quite close so they are easily identified when further away.

Naseby Church Spire: The spire is relatively modern, but a useful marker to determine the relation between the village and the viewpoint. It can frequently be seen above the treeline (SP 689782). At the time of the battle the church only had the tower.

Naseby church and churchyard with, beyond, the brick-fronted, rebuilt Shuckburgh House.

One of two remaining cob houses. The gable end, near the road, has been rebuilt in brick but the rest of the structure is traditional.

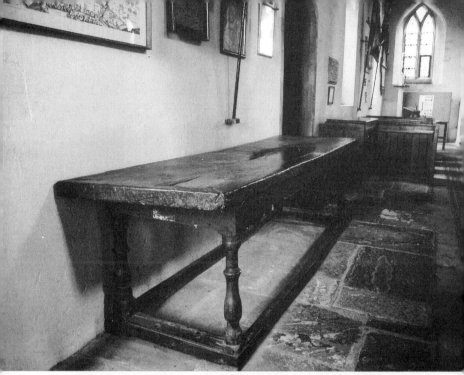

The oak dining table in Naseby church. King Charles's Life Guards were suprised by Parliamentarian cavalry whilst sitting eating supper at this table. There are other relics from the battle.

While in and around Naseby village the visitor can find a number of things to see. Except for the spire, the church is unaltered, though restored. Inside, against the north wall, a long oak table stands. Of this John Mastin writes in his 1792 history of the parish that an antiquarian of his acquaintance visiting Shuckburgh House had the following traditional account from two old gentlewomen, the tenants.

'A party of the King's life guards were surprised by Ireton, as they were sitting down to supper at this very table, the evening before the battle. Yes, Sir, at this very table.'

Shuckburgh House used to stand across the road from the church and it is known that a party of Royalists soldiers were taken by surprise in Naseby by Parliamentarian cavalry on the evening of 13 June, so this may well be true. The table was returned to the village early in the 20th century and was kept in the Reading Rooms before being moved here.

Shuckburgh House was rebuilt with a brick front before Mastin's time. He reports that Mr Ashby pulled down 'the venerable old, but sombrous, seat of the Shuckburghs' in 1773 and used the materials to build a farmhouse, the house that stands there today, south of the much more recent Fitzgerald Arms.

Behind a low wall north of the road junction outside this pub a curious pyramid of iron marks the source of the River Avon. It rarely runs with water nowadays this far up. The marker can be seen from the public pavement without intruding on the landowner's privacy.

Two cob houses survive in the village. They are in the High Street which runs parallel, and to the east of, the through road from Cold Ashby to Clipston. Both are painted white and thatched. The more recent, in the centre of the village, is built along the line of the road and modern thatched houses opposite attempt to echo its beauty. The older house stands gable-end on to the High Street further south, near to the junction with the Guilsborough and Thornby roads. Between the two houses is the length of road photographed in 1855 and shown in Chapter 4, page 79.

Communication Masts: There are two which are generally visible on the southern side of the area. The most useful is immediately south of the A14 north-east of Naseby on the track which is all that remains of the Kelmarsh road, east of the Parliamentarian viewpoint at the start of the day (SP 705792). A second mast is at Honey Hill, west of Cold Ashby (SP 641708), on the high land beyond the marshy meadows west of Naseby.

Mill Hill Farm: The farm stands south of the Parliamentary lines at the start of the battle (SP 684792). (Photograph page 99.)

Prince Rupert's Farm: This marks the western end of the Royalist infantry position at the start of the formal phase of the battle (SP 681809). (Photograph page 85.)

Dust Hill Farm: The Royalist left wing of cavalry formed up east of here (SP 688808) on a line through the wood, Long Hold Spinney, which was not planted at that time. (Photograph page 96.)

Lowe Farm: On the Sibbertoft to Clipston road (SP 691822) west of the Nobold closes, east of the Royalist baggage train and south west of Moot Hill and Wadborough. (Photograph page 115.)

The Royal Observer Corps Visual Reporting Post: On the hilltop west of the Clipston to Marston Trussel road and east of Wadborough (SP 702828) a hollow cube in red brick was built for World War II enemy aircraft spotters. For information about it see www.subbrit.org.uk. It can be seen, in association with a line of whispy poplar trees, from a long way off and also offers the visitor a prime viewpoint. (Photograph page 137).

There are, of course, many other features that the keen observer will identify and use, but these few are especially useful.

PRE-BATTLE CAMPAIGN MANOEUVRES (see chapter 2, page 37)

Parliament forces: Although it is obviously possible to track Fairfax from Oxford to Newport Pagnell and on via Stoney Stratford to Northampton, the first place welcoming to the imagination and to serious consideration of army movement is Kislingbury, west of Northampton and south of the A45 road to Daventry. The River Nene passes under the medieval bridge on the north side of the village (SP 699598) and it was over this bridge that the army marched on the morning of 13 June, shortly

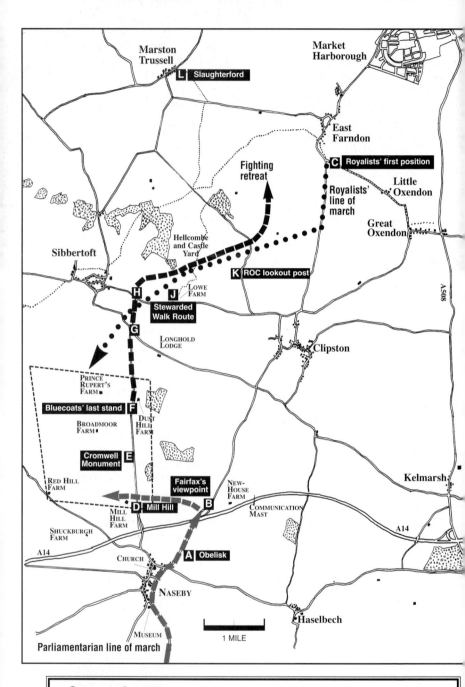

Suggested route

Arrange to visit the **Naseby Battle Museum** at Purlieu Farm (see page 156). Then perhaps a visit to **Naseby Church** to view the table. A chronological order of visit is either points **A**, **B** and **C** or alternatively, **C**, **B** and **A**, then **D** to **L** in alphabetical order. The Parliamentarian baggage train side trip (page 145-6) is best made when in Naseby village (see text page 131).

The Royal Observer Corps, Second World War, post provides an excellent platform from which to view the line of the Royalist retreat and the last stand of the Royalists on Wadborough.

after Cromwell had arrived with his Ironsides. North of the bridge a footpath bears away to the left, the north west, towards Harpole across a field in which a slightly raised causeway can be detected under the grass. The ridge that carries the Roman road from Duston on the outskirts of Northampton to Whilton, near to the site of Bannaventa on Watling Street (A5), can be seen beyond Harpole.

On the night of 12-13 June Fairfax was out and about in the rain, probing west but almost certainly south of the river. Today the Nene Way, a waymarked walk, passes through the village and heads for Bugbrooke and the Heyfords; much the route of Fairfax's reconnaissance.

Just which way the troops went from Kislingbury is uncertain. They were paraded for inspection, but the water meadows north of the river were not likely to have been suitable after the rain of the previous two days and there was clear space up on Harpole Common. (See map page 49). The Common lay to the north of the Roman road to Nobottle between Spring Lane in the east, on the outskirts of New Duston, and a now disused road further west which led to Harlestone, surviving today as a bridleway along part of its length. From here they made their way to Guilsborough to the north. There is no reason to suppose they travelled in a single column, but the artillery train must have followed the most solid surface they could find to avoid bogging down. They might well have taken the Roman road to the turn for Little Brington and plodded north, leaving the Spencer estate at Althorp on their right. Meanwhile others could well have gone the other side of the Park and even taken the road through Spratton and Creaton rather than the East Haddon, Ravensthorpe and Coton route.

On the morning of 14 June Fairfax had his men on the road early, for Ireton had stumbled on Royalists at Naseby the night before. The challenge was to select the most effective route off the ridge on which Guilsborough stands, to negotiate the valley bottom before gaining the ridge on which the Leicester road (A5199) runs and then cross the next stream to take one of the roads up a ridge to Naseby. In thinking about this it is necessary mentally to delete Hollowell Reservoir, east of Guilsborough, and allow for improved drainage of agricultural land in the last 350-odd years. Of all possible routes the Cold Ashby to Naseby road seems the least attractive, having, as it would have done, a long final run across marshy meadows which the early nineteenth century canal and its associated reservoir have dried out. Either of the remaining routes, direct or via Thornby, would bring them to the southern corner of Naseby village (pages 60-62).

Royalist forces: Having travelled from Leicester to Market Harborough, the Royalists, according to the Parliamentarian Luke, made their next rendezvous at Cold Ashby, passing through Kelmarsh on the way. They must, therefore, have brought their wheeled transport up the road to Naseby close by the communications mast and into the village on the road past the windmill, now the site of the obelisk. Their route to Daventry could have been either by way of Long Buckby or of Watford. The need to "rendezvous" at Cold Ashby suggests they did not travel in a single column and that the weather was dry enough for them to get their wagons across the low road from Naseby.

The camp at Daventry was set up on Borough Hill, the site of a huge Bronze Age ringwork with later fortifications, including Iron Age and Roman works, within it. It covers the entire hilltop east of the town and was crowned with radio masts until a single, towering mast was erected in their place at the southern end of the ancient enclosure. If approaching on the A45 from Weedon and Northampton, you turn north at the first roundabout as for Kilsby via the A361, the eastern ring road. At the next roundabout a right turn as for Southbrook brings you very soon to a road bearing off right and rustically signed "Welcome to Borough Hill." The single track road with passing places climbs to the top of the hill where, as the Royal Commission on Historical Monuments has it, "a continuous process of destruction and mutilation has affected the site". Parking is to the right, passing under a metal beam fixed to prevent unauthorized entry by large vehicles. The place has had its share of ravers and travellers in the past. From the top of this area, close to a flat-topped brick structure, a path leads anti-clockwise round the radio mast. Gorse or furze bushes line the old rampart and ditch fortification which still survives on this flank, and from the two benches along the path views can be had south east towards Weedon and even to Northampton if the day is clear, and east towards Norton's church tower, beyond a minor mast on the hillside, Watling Street and the M1 motorway. The A45 towards Coventry, from which the Banbury and Oxford road branches, is overlooked to the south. The strength and advantage of the position are evident (photograph page 43).

138

On the minor road from Daventry to Newnham, to the south, running across a bridge over the A45, the old windmill on Newnham Hill has been converted into a viewing tower. A footpath starts from the bottom of the hill, near the A45, and another from a lay-by near a stile at the top; either approach can be used. The tower, which is kept locked, affords superb views and from it the relationship between the camp on Borough Hill and the country east towards Northampton and south towards Oxford can be assessed. Access is free; the key to the tower can be borrowed on making a refundable deposit of £5 at the Daventry Tourist Information Centre and Museum, Moot Hall, Market Square (telephone 01327 300277 for opening times).

The route back to Market Harborough could not be one to risk contact with Fairfax's scouts and raiders, so the Royalists struck north. Ogilby's Britannia has a route map on which a road is shown with a curious kink in it; it heads roughly north, then east, then north once more before finally heading east on the northern side of the Welland. It may be that the road crossed the north-south tributary of the River Nene at Long Buckby or Watford, but a route avoiding the rivulet altogether lies through Ashby St Ledgers, just east of the road to Kilsby, and on to Crick, crossing Watling Street where the modern M45 from junction 17 goes under the older road. Otherwise it would be necessary to come through Watford and climb what is now a gated road to Crick. From Crick the route is easy; to Yelvertoft and, turning left there, through Clay Coton to Stanford on Avon, north of the modern A14. Stanford Hall now stands west of the river, which flows from north to south at this point. In Charles I's time the manor was on a now vacant site across the road from the church, next to the river; a convenient place to pause for dinner. The modern bridge carries the road to Swinford past the new Hall, built between 1697 and 1700, and the southern side of its park. Alongside the road bridge, to the north, the church side, King Charles's Bridge stands, semi-ruinous (photograph page 52). It is a charming, narrow causeway of brick, unsuitable for carts or carriages. The wheeled traffic of the King's train must, therefore, have gone by way of Catthorpe, to the west, and the entire force then moved east through North Kilworth and Husband's Bosworth to Lubenham and Market Harborough.

The radio mast on Borough Hill, Daventry, standing within the rampart and ditch defence. The mast permits visitors to identify Borough Hill Fort from a considerable distance.

THE BATTLE: PRELIMINARY POSITIONS (see Chapter 3, page 55)

Parliamentarians' positions

The Parliamentary forces were marching in pursuit of their enemies, whose rearguard they reckoned they had encountered at Naseby on the evening of 13 June. Their route to Market Harborough, where they supposed Charles I to be, lay either through Clipston or Kelmarsh or, perhaps, both. The former was acceptable for a cavalry and maybe an infantry advance, but wheeled transport would go the way the Royalists had come a few days before, along the Kelmarsh ridge.

The Obelisk – Viewpoint A: The highest point here is the windmill mound where the commemorative obelisk now stands opposite a layby for parking between Naseby village and the bridge over the A14 road (SP 694784) on the way to Clipston. Trees obscure the view from here, but to the north west (at right angles to the line of the road) Mill Hill Farm can be seen. Between this site and the A14 the ground dips significantly before rising to a lesser crest and in this area small groups of musket shot have been found, suggesting accidental loss rather than use in combat. If Fairfax and Cromwell went further forward to peer towards Market Harborough, this may be where Skippon first started organizing the arriving troops in battalia, out of the sight of Royalist eyes.

North of the A14 – Viewpoint B: The road to Clipston has been diverted slightly to cross the new bridge required by the A14 and, once over the bridge, it makes a gentle right curve before coming left to pick up the old line north-eastwards. At this point there is a farm gateway on the left (north west) near which, with care, one can park (SP 698791). From here the view to the north embraces both the area east of Sibbertoft over which the Royalists advanced and then retreated and the area in which they assembled early on 14 June.

Wadborough Hill is due north, but is more easily identified by looking a little to the west, the left, to see the white buildings of Lowe Farm on the horizon. Immediately to their right is Castle Yard, the site of the motte and bailey, crowned with a

The Obelisk on the Clipston road, photographed in the 1920s when new trees had just been planted around it. The trees virtually conceal the Obelisk today.

Lowe Farm   Moot Hill   Wadborough Hill

Seen from viewpoint B, Lowe Farm, Moot Hill and Wadborough.

Wellingtonia (redwood) tree, and Sibbertoft wood. Then there are few isolated trees and a long stretch of wood, all just beyond Moot Hill where the King's standard is said to have flown. The woods descend the hillside into the valley beyond Nobold closes and the land then rises to the open field of Wadborough. The next valley contains the woods in the gully around which the fleeing Royalists passed to the east, then comes the hill on which, outlined against the hills north of the Welland River in the distance, the square brick block of the Observer Corps lookout stands and just to the right of it the rising line of tall, thin, pointed, poplar trees that adjoin the single-track Clipston to Marston Trussell road.

Royalists' positions

Further east the initial Royalist position can be seen, beyond the village of Clipston which runs at right angles across the line of sight, down in the valley. Starting from the right, the east, the spire of Clipston church can be seen and beyond it a line of trees along the top of the distant ridge, with another range of hills behind in the far distance. Running the eye to the west, the left, along the tree-topped ridge the bulk of the buildings of Little Oxendon Farm is seen. They stand in the centre of what was the enclosure of Little Oxendon and the solid bulk of trees to the west ceases where the enclosure reached its western limit, that is, the eastern limit of the ground available to Prince Rupert to draw up his forces. The continuing line of occasional trees marks the course of the East Farndon to Little Oxendon road on its ridge: the rear of the Royalist position. Taking into account the fact that the trees in the valley would not have obscured the view at the time, and that the early morning sun, if there was any, would be behind and to the right of the observer standing where you are now, it is clear that Fairfax and Cromwell would have had an excellent view of their enemies while their own troops were down behind them towards Naseby.

From this point it is possible to drive east past New-house Farm on the Kelmarsh road, now very minor road, and explore the route from the main Market Harborough to Northampton road. The communications mast stands alongside this road.

From this position on the Clipston Road a move west to the battle positions north of Mill Hill Farm would not be hard to execute. Immediately west of the viewpoint at the field gate the hedgeline leads the eye to another field, and beyond that the tops of trees growing in a gully that falls steeply north (right) can be seen. This is part of the remains of the confused slope Cromwell thought the Royalists would never attack, but most of it has been bulldozed smooth in the last century. Between that and Naseby, though now cut by the A14, runs a broad, accommodating ridge, Gibbs Hill – an easy road to the new position Fairfax took up.

The Royalist advance

The Royalist forces came from Market Harborough by way of Bloodyman's Ford and Charles fled this way, and was almost captured, at the end of the battle. Leaving the centre of Market Harborough on the A4304 in the direction of Husband's Bosworth, the road passes a hospital on the right before coming to a turning south, left, for East Farndon. This crosses the River Welland on a bridge that stands where the ford was in 1645 (SP 728869) on the west side of Welland Park. The road continues to the village of East Farndon and makes its twisting way to the top of the ridge. The church is on the left, the east, of the road shortly before a turn to the left as it leaves the village to go eastwards towards the road to Clipston and its junction with the ridge road to Little Oxendon. To the right, the west, the hillside falls steeply to the flood plain of the Welland.

The Royalist Right – viewpoint C: At the junction of the Clipston and Little Oxendon roads (SP 717845) a footpath leads north from which the church on its little eminence can be seen. Allowing again for a landscape without trees, it can be understood that the image of "a Hill whereupon a Chappell stood" would endure in Slingsby's mind. From this point it is possible at the time of writing to have access to the East Farndon Pastures conservation walk, at the northern end of which gorse or furze is still to be seen. Detailed information can be had on www.countrywalks.org.uk.

A drive along the Little Oxendon road shows the extent to which the Royalists could get a glimpse, but not a thorough overview, of the

The churchyard of Great Oxendon church is well below the ridgetop. From here there is a waymarked walk to Little Oxendon deserted village.

Line of trees on the
East Farndon Road

Little Oxendon

Seen from viewpoint B, Little Oxendon Farm and the tree-marked East Farndon to Great Oxendon road, the rear of the Royalists' first position.

Parliamentary forces on the Clipston road at Naseby. The communications mast east of New-house Farm next to the A14 can be seen to the left and the spire of Naseby Church over a clump of trees to the right (photograph page 57). The A14, with its stream of high-sided trucks, can only be seen in parts and, as inspection from near the obelisk shows, the land could conceal a large body of men from view from the East Farndon ridge. What it is hard to see from here is the re-entrant to the west, past Jugsholme Farm, which prevented the Royalists from marching a direct line to Moot Hill from this position and necessitated a move towards Clipston before turning west. Moot Hill is, however, visible from the forward slope on the right and so a standard planted on top of it would have been a useful guide to troops moving towards new positions south of Sibbertoft (photograph page 58). Travel across the valley to Naseby involves going up and down over little humps and a final, steep climb up to viewpoint B. The visibility of the trucks on the A14 varies as you go, giving an idea of the problems of reconnoitering this terrain (diagram page 65).

At the western end of the ridge Great Oxendon stands on the main road north from Northampton (A508) and the church is north of the village itself, just to the west of the main road up a little access road. A visit shows that it stands below the ridge line and is hard to square with Slingsby's impression of a hill with a chapel on it. It is possible to walk from here to the site of the deserted village of Little Oxendon, guided by a map at the stile in the churchyard, and to see well-preserved ridge and furrow. The deserted village can also be reached from the ridge road by a path detailed on www.countrywalks.org.uk.

THE BATTLE – THE FORMAL PHASE (see Chapter 4, page 71)

The Parliamentary army moved over to a new position at first on Cloister, the hill north of Mill Hill on which the farm of that name stands. An appreciation of this has to be formed only from what can be seen from the

143

road as there are no public footpaths to help.

Behind the Parliamentary lines – viewpoint D: It is possible, again with great care, to park where the Sibbertoft road from Naseby crosses Mill Hill, near the drive to Mill Hill Farm (SP 686793), leaving space for the movement of farm vehicles both on the road and through the gates. It is necessary to walk up and down to get an appreciation of the terrain as trees and hedges get in the way of a single view. To the east (right facing to Sibbertoft) the land rises to Gibbs Hill and in front it falls away into a valley through which a little stream flows east then north around Paisnell Spinney. From the forward slope of the Gibbs Hill/Mill Hill ridge it is possible to oversee all the land to the crest of Cloister and beyond to Sulby Hedges, Dust Hill and, except for some dead ground where the Cromwell Monument is, much of Broadmoor. (photograph, page 82) The spinney is a later planting as are the hedges and trees, so it could be that Cromwell supervised the operations of the right wing of horse from Gibbs Hill's northern face, Fodder Hill as the field is called. What can also be appreciated from this road is how the hill to the north rises and then ripples on before coming to what Sprigge called the ledge of the hill, the little steepness just south of the Monument. The principal finds of shot were on the top of this feature, one field south of the Monument. The shooting took place at short range, for the Royalists had already clambered up the 'ledge' before the two sides saw each other and they were soon engaged hand-to-hand.

In front of the Parliamentary line – viewpoint E: There is a lay- bay for three cars on the forward slope of Cloister and a footpath leads to the Cromwell Monument, a walk that is only about one sixth of the width of the infantry front and one ninth of the distance to the line of Sulby Hedges, the limit of the Parliamentarian line. The natural thing is to look north, over Broadmoor. Look south instead! Remove the hedge in your imagination. This is the ledge, the step up to a lesser slope to the summit of Cloister. The attacking Royalist might not yet see his enemy from here, perhaps only the heads of officers on horseback and the tops of massed pikes. The fallow field's scrubby grass and scattered bushes underfoot, the two sides panted forward towards each other, closing to a point near the far, southern, hedge, having exchanged two bursts of musketry in that time. Along the hedge behind the monument to the west, away from the road, the ground dips, indicating the re-entrant which channelled the Royalists into a wedge and split the Parliamentarian front. Skippon's men were cut off from the main body, Waller's fell back and the front collapsed into the reserves, back towards the valley under Mill Hill.

Looking northwards, Broadmoor Farm is to the left on the valley floor and to the right of it, up on Dust Hill, is Prince Rupert's Farm. A farm road leads back to the Sibbertoft road and right of that is Dust Hill Farm. It is hard to see clearly, but the line of the farm road projected leftwards, to the west, bisects the sight-line through Broadmoor Farm in the enclosure beyond Sulby Hedges in which Okey's men were first fired on by Rupert's

The Monument dedicated to Oliver Cromwell, looking north east. The Sibbertoft road is marked by a line of trees running right to left and, to their left, the second hedge marks the parish boundary. Here the road curves to the right and the field to its left is where the Bluecoats made their stand. On the skyline to the right is Long Hold Spinney.

musketeers and driven back south down the slope (see photograph, page 83). On the other flank, this side, west, of the Sibbertoft road, the field this side of, i.e. south of, the farm road is the position finally held, 'like a wall of brasse' by Rupert's Bluecoats (see photograph, page 87).

Leaving the car in the lay-by, a walk back up the road towards Naseby brings you to a gate on the east of the road. If you miss it you pass a cart track and a derilict cottage, so turn back to the gate and look east. The hilltop beyond the hedge, the next field over, is Lodge Hill, the site of the rabbit warren, so you are looking along the front on which Langdale's Northern Horse and Cromwell's cavalry clashed. Across the valley to the north on the east of the road is Dust Hill Farm and Longhold Spinney, a wood not yet planted at the time. Langdale's men formed up over there.

The Royalist line – viewpoint F: Opportunities to park once over the parish boundary are difficult to find. The road from Naseby crosses Broadmoor, passes the farm road to Broadmoor Farm and, at the end of the next field, kinks a little to the right; that's the parish boundary. From here on you are following a road that existed in 1645 and it feels like it! If the weather is dry it may be possible to pull off on the roadside near the entrance to Prince Rupert's and Dust Hill farms. If in doubt leave the car at the monument lay-by and walk. From the roadside on Dust Hill (SP 686808) the Parliamentarian line can be seen, (see photograph, page 94) but note particulary the treetops and see how much concealed terrain there is on the far side of the valley beyond Cloister, making Slingsby's remark 'they lay without our sight, having ye Hill to cover ym' entirely understandable. It was in this field, next to, and off to the west of, the road that musket shot was found in profusion across the bottom of the slope and pistol balls halfway up to the top, then, to the north of the farm road, musket balls once more; evidence of the Bluecoats' defence against the pistol-packing cavalry attacking both from in front and from behind.

Parliament's baggage – a side-trip: As the position of the baggage which Rupert attacked is uncertain, there are a number of places one ought to look. Carvell's Lane leaves Naseby village from the centre of the western side, opposite the Wesleyan chapel, curving past the houses to become a dead-straight enclosure road down on the levels. To the north the land rises beyond the little stream that is actually the River Avon, beloved of tourists at Stratford. Clearly this area is totally unsuited to wagons. From the north-western corner of the village the road leaves past the Fitzgerald Arms and a new housing development to kink left, west, and drop down a slope. At the kink a band of trees, Clothill Spinney, goes due north alongside what might well have been the access road to Turmoore Field and the battlefield in 1645. If the artillery train came through the village it would surely have avoided going down the slope and would follow the cart track north. If it came anti-clockwise through or round Naseby, it must have followed the track along the edge of Shepshoks Field or come along the road north of the church to the Turmoore Field road. In any case, it arrives just about where the Sibbertoft road crosses the A14 and stops near here or pushes on along the southern side of Mill Hill for a way to the extension of the raised land called Fenny Hill. Finally, we have to remember that the artillery train is guarded and there are also references to 'plundering the baggage' with no guarantee that the same trains are being spoken of. On the other hand, if the train halted south of the village the possible location is found by leaving the Cold Ashby road within the village by way of Nutcote and taking the Thornby road to the right (see map, page 108). Opposite the farm road to Oak Farm (SP685772) to the east is a flat little field, Mill Field, overlooking the steep-sided valley south of the village. Looking back, to the north to Mill Hill Farm, to the village itself, and to the east of it, an area very attractive to wagon drivers struggling up from Thornby can be seen. Fleeing Parliamentary horse would have come from a point west of Mill Hill Farm and from here their destination, Northampton, can be seen to the south. One could ask why Rupert's horse did not return to the battlefield by the easier road over Gibbs Hill and Mill Hill instead of retracing their steps over the route to the west. Might they have been deterred by a skirmish with a force holding this position south of the village and preventing their taking a route anti-clockwise around it? Lacking better evidence for any single one of these locations, it's anybody's guess!

THE BATTLE – THE FIGHTING RETREAT (see Chapter 5, page 105)

The evidence of the retreat continues. Metal detection has established that, from Dust Hill, fighting took place all the way north along the Sibbertoft road. Shot has been found on the west close to the road and on the east there is a band of shot along the field edge in the area between the only two houses on the road. There may be more to be found under pasture land on the east.

The Royal baggage – viewpoints G and H: At the point at which the Naseby to Sibbertoft road meets the road up from Kelmarsh a footpath carries on due north, possibly on the line of an earlier road heading for the castle. It is possible to park at the south end of the path (SP 685819) and walk towards the gate on the far side of the field. The footpath is at times ploughed over, but navigation is not hard; just aim for the gate. The area to the right of the footpath between the road and a point about halfway across the field was heavy with shot, some of it, at the southern end, larger than the usual musket 12-bore ball. If this was from swivel-guns mounted on baggage wagons, the possibility is that the train was between this point and Lowe Farm, to the north east on the Clipston road, bringing down fire on the advancing enemy. Walking on north between the paddocks on the other side of the gate brings you to the Clipston road, along which the line of musket balls continues; the completion of the arc of fire from the baggage train directed at the enveloping Parliamentarian force.

Before returning to fetch the car, if car-borne, look beyond the road to the north (viewpoint H, SP 686824), where a sign marked 'bridleway' points back the way you came, to see one line of flight. The land falls away and to the left it leads into a tree- lined gully. Musket shot was found along a line from the road to that gully, Hellcoombe, in which the graves of cavaliers are said to have been found. To the right the trees rise and one in particular is prominent. It stands in Castle Yard, the site of the motte and bailey castle. To the right again a circular spinney stands on a little hillock and there are woods and another field to the right of that. The field to the right, the east, is King's Close which is the top of Moot Hill. More musket shot was found, in some profusion, across from the road, around the near side, the south side, of the spinney and in some concentration towards the top of the hill on the western side, fire from the top of Moot Hill which is another viewpoint – J (there is no I).

Stands and slaughter – viewpoint J and a walk: On the opposite side of the road, the north, to Lowe Farm on the Clipston road a Conservation Walk starts. The complete circuit is something over three miles (five kilometres). There is limited parking here, next to the gateway (SP 691823) and detailed information on the walk itself can be had on www.countrywalks.org.uk (where it is curiously listed as 'Land at Marston Trussell') showing how it goes through to Dick's Hill (the Clipston to Marston Trussell road). There is also a map on the gatepost at the start. The path angles to the right across the first field to a gap in the hedge into King's Close. The summit of Moot Hill can be seen marked with an Ordnance Survey triangulation pillar. The path goes down the hedgeside to the right and turns left at the bottom.

On the top of the hill and the forward slope to the west, where the hedge

147

runs, musket shot was found, but down the hill into the valley to the right pistol shot prevails, the evidence of cavalry pursuit of fleeing or retreating infantry. Before walking down into the valley, look over the hedge to the right towards the road into the field east, downhill, of the one just walked over. This is Englands, a corruption of Inlands, one of the two Nobold enclosures. The road at the time of the battle passed between this and the village enclosure to the south, just as it does today. We know that the Royal baggage had to make its way along the road from East Farndon to Clipston and then up here so it is very likely that it was still arriving as the Royalists fell back. It is not hard to imagine the confusion as those in front tried to turn about and those behind pressed ignorantly onwards. Meanwhile those who had already arrived were caught, unable to go south about the closes because of the advance of Fairfax's men, or north because that was a battlefield, or down the road because that was a traffic jam. So they tried to

Viewpoints J and K. Lowe Farm is on the left, south of the Sibbertoft to Clipston road. The walk starts past the reservoir and turns right down the hedge as soon as it enters King's Close in which the Moot Hill triangulation pillar stands. It then follows the parish boundary (dotted) northwards. Point K is close to the Welland/Nene watershed on the road right centre. The fields comprising the old Nobold closes are tinted to aid identification. CROWN COPYRIGHT

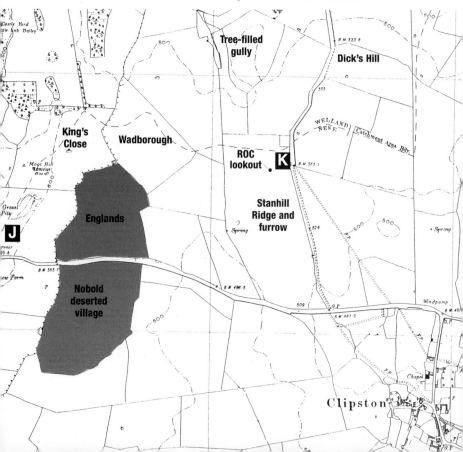

Gulley

Marston Trussell

Likely location from where King Charles viewed the last charge of the battle by his cavalry

The field gate near the poplars, close to viewpoint K. Possibly King Charles's view of his cavalry's last charge in the battle to oppose the pursuit coming from Wadborough on the left.

cross Englands to a presumed gate in the far side, a bottleneck, and here they were caught, slashed across the face, robbed or killed. The only finds in this field have been of contemporary coins. This scenario cannot be proved, but makes sense.

Continuing to the foot of Moot Hill the path turns north along the hedge, which is also the parish boundary. Here one of the densest concentrations of musket balls in all the battlefield was found. The hill up to the right is Wadborough, and on the side of it, above the hedge, the band of bullets continues. From above, on Wadborough itself, the last of the King's musketeers must have made their last, stubborn stand, explaining why the western side of the valley has an equal concentration of shot. The exchange of fire was ferocious. The hilltop is scattered with a dusting of shot, and then patches of bullets are found down the other side, eastwards around a tree-filled gulley and away towards Market Harborough. The last scene of the battle, viewpoint K, can be reached either by continuing the walk to Dick's Hill, the road to the north, and turning right, or by returning to the car opposite Lowe Farm and driving.

The Royal Observers Corps Visual Reporting Post – viewpoint K:
From the Clipston to Sibbertoft road a single-track road climbs the hill north towards Marston Trussell. On the top of it a line of poplar trees stands at right angles to the road, a useful landmark from afar. There is space to park without blocking passing places for other traffic. From the field gate next to the poplars (SP 703828), looking back towards Sibbertoft, the eastern side of Wadborough is seen with Moot Hill beyond. At the foot of the slope on which you are standing lies the gully full of trees and on the near side of it musket balls mark the last efforts of the Royalist cavalry to slow the enemy advance.

A few steps back towards Clipston, on the same side of the road, a stile carries a stewardship waymark (valid to September 2007) and in the field beyond is the red brick cube of the Observer Corps lookout, which includes a Cold War Underground Monitoring Post, (SP 702827). From it a

Looking southward from the Observer Corps lookout, K. Naseby church spire projects above the trees, after a clear space, Clothill Spinney can be seen. The next wood is Paisnell Spinney and to its right, before Long Hold Spinney, Mill Hill Farm can just be seen.

remarkable view of almost the whole proceedings of 14 June 1645 can be had. It is as well to come to this point at the end of your tour because it will be easier to identify landmarks previously seen at close quarters.

Looking back towards and beyond the road from which you have just come, the hill on which East Farndon stands and the tree-marked road to Little Oxendon can be seen – the Royalists' first position. Below is the tree-filled gully they would have had to march around by the south to come across past this postion and also up the road from Clipston to Sibbertoft. Turning clockwise, the communications mast on the A14 stands on the skyline and from that it is possible to figure out the Parliamentarian positions just this side of it. Clockwise again and the spire of Naseby church appears, as does Mill Hill Farm. Most of the first phase battlefield is obscured by trees of more recent planting, but Lowe Farm marks the start of the Sibbertoft plateau from which it would have been possible to see men on Cloister, north of Mill Hill. From Lowe Farm the line of final retreat and flight lies before you. Away to the right is Marston Trussell and turning clockwise some more, the route to Market Harborough beneath East Farndon's site on the hill above. This landscape cradled British democracy.

The Welland Valley – viewpoint L: Apart from Bloodyman's Ford, only one location of the flight is worth a visit, Marston Trussell (see pages 118 and 119). Dick's Hill (page 136) joins the Sibbertoft to Marston Trussell road north of Marston Lodge Farm. It is worth pausing just before the junction to look back at the exit of Hellcoombe from the hills and to appreciate how steeply the land falls to the flood plain of the River Welland. The road into Marston Trussell now runs well to the east of the line of 1645 because the stream was dammed to form a lake when the Hall was built in the 19th

Looking westward from the Observer Corps lookout, K. Above the pool of water, on the skyline, the white buildings of Lowe Farm and, dark on the hillside above the pale valley floor, Englands. Right of Lowe Farm the isolated trees on the horizon are on the southern edge of King's Close on Moot Hill with Sibbertoft Wood right of that and Wadborough this side of it.

century but it still joins the main street, Lubenham Road, west of the old through road's left turn at the point now marked with a public footpath sign. It went north for a short distance before turning right behind the houses to go on its way as Harborough Road and today the footpath continues north at that point just as it did when the land was enclosed. What appeared to be the main road, the village road to the church, Pudding-bay-end [Pudding-bag-end], went no further than the modern church gate, (SP 694859) where there is room to park without blocking access to the neighbouring house. A public footpath still passes the church porch and leaves the graveyard by a stile beyond to bring you into the field known as Slawford (viewpoint L), just as shown on the enclosure map of 1815 (page 123). To the left is the site of the manor house and its moat, the corner of which abuts the north-eastern corner of the graveyard. The tributary of the Welland flows along the field edge to the right, the south, beyond which the hills near Sibbertoft can be seen. The naming of the field seems to have little connection with the credible story of men trapped in the dead-end road and would fit another story, which does not exist, about Royalists killed as they forded the rivulet south of the field, arriving from the battlefield on this footpath. Indeed, the name might have no connection with the battle at all.

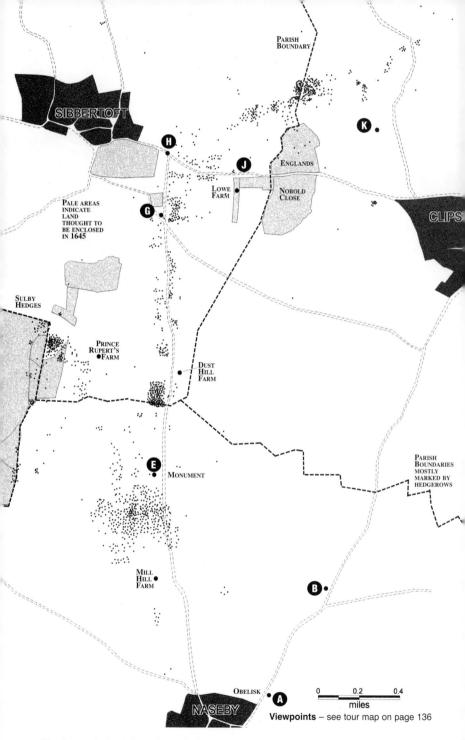

Musket and pistol shot found in Naseby, Sibbertoft and Clipston parishes.
© Peter Burton, Michael Westaway and Glenn Foard, 2002.

FURTHER READING

Readers requiring a more thorough and detailed account of the campaign are advised to read Glenn Foard's *Naseby: The Decisive Campaign* in which the findings of the metal detectorists, including two of the authors of this book, were first taken into account in the interpretation of the battle. At the time of writing Glenn Foard is working on a new book also likely to be of interest to be published in the *Theatre of War* series edited by Professor Richard Holmes and published by Cassell Military. For a sound general military history of the English Civil War, 1642-1651, see Stuart Reid's *All the King's Armies*. Contemporary writings are reproduced in Foard and in Peter Young's *Naseby 1645* as appendix material and are the sources of the quotations in this book. Well illustrated and precise accounts of weapons, dress and fighting methods are given in the Men-at-Arms and Elite series produced by Osprey Publishing. The New Model Army is the subject of Men-at-Arms No. 110 and the infantry of the English Civil War is dealt with in *Elite* No. 25 while the cavalry is the subject of *Elite* No. 27. The same publisher's Campaign series covers only the Battle of Edgehill at the time of writing, but Marston Moor and Naseby are to be expected.

References

Asquith, Stuart, *New Model Army 1645-60*, Men-at-Arms No. 110, London, Osprey Publishing, 1981.

Barriffe, Wiliam, ed. Keith Roberts, *Militarie Discipline: or the Young Artilleryman*, London, 1661 and Leigh-on-Sea, Partizan Press, 1988.

Clarendon, Edward Hyde, Earl of, ed. Roger Lockyer, *The History of the Great Rebellion*, London, Oxford University Press for the Folio Society, 1967.

Fiennes, Celia, ed. Christopher Morris, *The Illustrated Journeys of Celia Fiennes 1682-1712*, London, Webb & Bower/Michael Joseph.

Foard, Glenn, *Naseby: The Decisive Campaign*, Whitstable, Pryor Publications, 1995.

Goodfellow, Peter, *Medieval Bridges in Northamptonshire*, Northamptonshire Past and Present Vol VII No 3, Northamptonshire Record Society, 1985-86.

Grose, Francis, *Military Antiquities Respecting a History of the English Army*, Second Edition, London, Stockdale, 1812.

Mastin, John, *The History and Antiquities of Naseby*, Cambridge, Hodson, 1792.

Reid, Stuart, *All the King's Armies*, Staplehurst, Spellmount, 1998.

Roberts, Keith, *Soldiers of the English Civil War 1: Infantry*, Elite No. 25, London, Osprey Publishing, 1989.

Royal Commission on Historical Monuments England, *An Inventory of the Historical Monuments in the County of Northampton*, Vols III and IV, London, H.M.S.O., 1981.

Skelton, R. A., *Saxton's Survey of England and Wales*, Amsterdam, Nico Israel, 1974.

Taylor, Christopher, *Roads and Tracks of Britain*, London, Dent, 1979 and Orion, 1994.

Tincey, John, *Soldiers of the English Civil War 2: Cavalry*, Elite No. 27, London, Osprey Publishing, 1990.

Trevelyan, G. M., *English Social History* Vol 2, London, Longmans Green, 1942.

Whitaker, Harold, *Printed Maps of Northamptonshire*, Northampton, Northamptonshire Record Society, 1948.

Young, Peter, *The English Civil War, Men-at-Arms No.14*, London Osprey Publishing, 1973.

Young, Peter, *Naseby 1645*, London, Century Publishing, 1985.

MUSEUMS

Naseby Battle and Farm Museum

This long established museum houses a battlefield diorama with 850 model soldiers. The display shows three stages of the battle, which is described in a ten-minute commentary. Relics from the battlefield include swords, helmets, breast-plate, musket and cannon balls. Also on display are maps, letters etc.

Open Bank Holiday Sundays and Mondays   2 pm to 5 pm.
Other times by special arrangement.
Telephone: Janet Hillyer 01604 740662
Admission fee £2.00
Purlieu Farm, Naseby, Northamptonshire

Cromwell Museum

Oliver Cromwell was born in Huntingdon in 1599 and went to school in this building. The museum is devoted to the life of Cromwell and the Parliamentary side in the Civil War. There are portraits of the leading figures of the time and items that once belonged to the Lord Protector. The exhibit also includes coins and medals.

April to October: Tuesday to Friday, 1pm to 4pm.
Saturday and Sunday 11am to 1pm and 2pm to 4pm
November to March: Tuesday to Friday 11am to 1pm and 2pm to 5pm.
Saturday 11am to 1pm and 2pm to 4pm
Sunday 2pm to 4pm
Grammar School Walk, Market Hill, High Street, Huntingdon PE18 6NR
Telephone 01480 375830.

Oliver Cromwell's House

This was the family home of Oliver Cromwell and the museum deals not only with the man himself but also with the broader context of 17th Century life.

April to September: Monday to Sunday and Bank Holidays 10am to
5.30pm
October to March: Monday to Saturday 10am to 5pm.
Sunday 11.15 to 4pm

29 St Mary's Street, Ely.
Telephone 01353 662062

Rockingham Castle

Rockingham played a major role in the Civil War and was taken and beseiged by both Cavaliers and Roundheads.
Easter Sunday to 30 September: Sundays and Thursdays and Bank Holiday Mondays and
1.30pm to 5.30pm
Near Corby, Northants (Exit 15 off M1)
Telephone 0536 770240

Daventry: Tourist Information Centre and Museum
Moot Hall, Market Square, Daventry. Telephone 01327 300277

Market Harborough: Tourist Information Centre and Museum
Adam and Eve Street, Market Harborough. Telephone 01858 821270

Northampton: Central Museum and Art Gallery
Guildhall Road, Northampton Telephone 01604 2398548
Abington Museum **Abington Park, Northampton** Telephone 01604 631454

ENGLISH CIVIL WAR SOCIETY

The King's Army

The Roundheads

We aim to bring this turbulent and exciting period of history to life, combining history, live action and public education. The Parliamentarian and King's forces have their own command structures which combine to offer both the spectacular and everyday activities of the 17th Century.

Our Living History displays portray social interaction, civil administration, food, clothing, entertainment complete with accurate reproduction of the artifacts of the time. Our members are practiced in military skills such as cavalry, pike, musket, sword, cannon and battlefield supply, and many are able to offer researched background about daily life, history and religion of the period.

What we can offer event organisers:
We can tailor events to your requirements and budget from carnivals and fetes to county fairs at schools, Heritage sites and show grounds, supporting educational projects, local historical events and as a major attraction at fund raising events. The number of participants and authentic equipment can be matched to the event from the tens to the many hundreds.

To join us or enquire about hosting an event please contact:

ECWS, 70 Hailgate, Howden,
East Yorkshire DN14 7ST
Email: press@english-civil-war-society.org

The opportunity to take part in this exciting and rewarding hobby, learn the military and life skills of the time, take part in battle re-enactment and living histories, and join in the entertaining post event social activities, off-season training and banquets.

155

The Royal Armouries
– Leeds

Here is housed the largest and finest collection of arms and armour used in the English Civil Wars 1642 to 1651.

April to September:
Monday to Sunday
10.30am to
5.30pm

October to March:
Monday to Saturday
10am to 4.30pm.

**Armouries Drive, Leeds,
Yorkshire LS10 1LT**
Telephone 0113 220 1999

ADMISSION FREE AT LEEDS

Royal Armouries The White Tower
The Tower of London
Open: March to October
Sunday and Monday 10am to 6pm
Tuesday to Saturday 9am to 6pm
Open: November to February
Sunday and Monday 10am to 5pm
Tuesday to Saturday 9am to 5pm

Prince Rupert's Bluecoats – a company of musketeers during drill.

The Sealed Knot is a nationwide society which re-enacts battles, skirmishes and sieges of the English Civil Wars (1642-49) and seeks to portray ordinary life in the 17th Century in its 'Living History' displays.

These events stimulate public interest in the social and military events of this important period in English history and at the same time time help raise money for various charities, both local and national.

If you wish to participate on the battlefield you can join as a pikeman, musketeer, drummer, cannon crew, pioneer or matrose. Should you not wish to 'fight' you can join the Baggage Tryne and take part in pre-battle displays and cameos.

Children may also be part of the Baggage Tryne, but are not allowed on the battlefield until they are sixteen. There is an active Apprentices at Armes Corps for children aged 12-16.

PRINCE RUPERT'S BLEW REGIMENT OF FOOTE

HERTS/SOUTH BEDS	LONDON/SURREY/HAMPSHIRE	BUCKS/NORTH BEDS
STEVE PHILLIPS	**ARTHUR JACKSON**	**MARY HAWKINS**
01442 394909	**01689 819159**	**01908 564550**

INDEX

Italic entries refer to illustrations

The authors left to right: Peter Burton, Michael Westaway and Martin Marix Evans.

Peter Burton was born in Sibbertoft and has been searching the battlefield area for shot and equipment for more than fifteen years.

Michael Westaway's father farmed Prince Rupert's Farm and Michael, born in Naseby, has been researching the battlefield since boyhood.

Martin Marix Evans is a military historian with a particular interest in relating battlefield action to the realities of the terrain.